Magic Spells Of All Kinds

By Draja Mickaharic and several others

Including the famous Papa Jim

Gathered and presented by

Draja Mickaharic

Lulu Inc.

Morrisville, North Carolina
United States Of America

First Published in 2008 By
Lulu, Inc.
860 Aviation Parkway
Morrisville, NC 27560

www.Lulu.com

Voice: 919-459-5858

Fax: 919-459-5867

ISBN

LCCN

Printed in the United States of America

Amatory Magic Or Love Spells

Attraction Spells

Magnet Oil may be used to attract material things, including a lover. Take a lodestone, and drop one drop of magnet oil on it for each year of your life and one more. Wrap the lodestone in a piece of paper on which your desire has been written. Carry the lodestone with you to draw what you wish to you.

Magnet Oil may also be used for healing. Dress a candle with magnet oil praying that it draw out malefic forces and draw in health.

An Attraction Bath

Steep equal quantities of Hyssop and Sweet balm in water, by keeping the mixture in the refrigerator for seven days. Add the herb and water to a tub bath, adding a teaspoon full of attraction oil. Pray over the bath for what is wanted. You may pray either for a specific person, for a lover, without specifying who, or you may pray for a marriage, either for marriage to a specific person or for marriage in general.

You should be aware that any spells done for either love or marriage, without mentioning a specific person, have a much better chance of success than spells done to draw a specific person to you.

An Attraction Perfume

Use a drop each of Amber oil, Sweet Pea oil, Jasmine Oil, Sandalwood Oil and White Rose Oil. Add perfume diluent to suit. Pray over the oil to attract the right person to you. Used successfully to attract a member of the opposite sex.

From Susan Tredway in NYC

A Bath For A Woman To Find A Lover

These baths are to be used by a woman only when there is no one on the horizon who has shown any interest in her. This is a series of five baths to be taken on five consecutive days. Each of the five baths consists of:

> Five sprigs of fresh parsley
> Five sticks of cinnamon
> A tablespoon of ground blackthorn bark
> ½ teaspoon of deer horn shavings

One Star anise

A teaspoon of ground (Powdered) Amanza Guapo

(Florida Boxwood or Balmony)

These herbs are put into boiling water and steeped, making them into a tea, and the mixture is allowed to cool. Once cool, a drop of mercury is added to the mixture, and a tablespoon of honey is stirred into the completed bath.

While in the tub, the woman should visualize the kind of man she is looking for, but without thinking of not particular man. She should remain in the tub seven minutes and immerse herself five times. Ideally, this bath may be taken on arriving home from work each day of the five days.

To Bring Heartbreak Into A Home

To cause a broken heart in a home, hide a peacock feather in the house. Usually when this spell is cast, the feather is put under a rug. However, it must always be hidden in some place where it is unlikely to be found. The cause of the heartbreak will begin within five days, and will usually last until the hidden peacock feather is found and disposed of by throwing into the running water of a stream or the ocean.

This spell is frequently used to encourage a man to leave his wife, or encourage a wife to leave her husband. When it is used for this purpose, the departing person will need time to recover from their heartbreak. The person who cast the spell should not be in a hurry to try and rope the other person in.

Iceland Spar Marriage Spell

Take a piece of Iceland spar, a crystal like quartz. Put the crystal into a white bowl. Underneath the Iceland spar, place the two names of the couple to be married, written on the same piece of paper with a heart drawn around the names. Give the Iceland spar a shot of grain alcohol or vodka, pouring it over the crystal. Pray that the obstacles to the marriage of the couple be removed, and that they marry. Feed the Iceland spar by pouring vodka or grain alcohol over it for seven days. After seven days, cover the bowl with a white cloth.

Once the marriage has occurred, feed the Iceland spar for another seven days, as a thank you offering for its assistance.

On the eighth day, wash the Iceland spar under cold water, take the paper away, and wash away the names. If the names won't wash off, dry the paper and then burn it, blowing the ashes to the four winds.

After the spar is washed, wrap it in a white cloth and put it into the bowl, saving it for the next use. Best time to begin this spell is during the waxing Moon.

To Separate A Couple

Make a vigil lamp, at the bottom of which is confusion and in tranquil perfume, to which is added: 7 pins, 7 needles, 7 nails, 7 cloves, a pinch of table salt, Precipatdo Roja (Red Mercuric Oxide), and mercury. The names of the couple are written crossed (X) on a piece of paper torn from a paper grocery bag and added to the top of the material in the oil lamp. Seven Grains of Paradise are put on top of the paper.

Oil is placed on top of the lamp, (Olive oil, peanut oil, or some other cooking oil are all satisfactory). The vigil lamp is to be burned until the separation of the couple is complete.

From Norma at the Arara Botanica
On Amsterdam Avenue in NYC

To Cause Anger And Argument Between Two People

Take the seeds of two dry hot peppers and write the names of the couple on two pieces of paper. Twist the seeds of one member of the couple in one paper, and the seeds of the other member of the couple in another paper. Place both papers on the stove, in a saucepan or frying pan, and heat them up. Do not allow the papers to burn, but heat them in the pan for a few moments. You can re-heat these twisted papers whenever you wish.

Traditional

One man put the twisted papers with the names of his boss and the boss's boss under a heat lamp for the entire time he was at work for two weeks. This ended in a fistfight between the two of them, which resulted in the police being called. The man's boss was fired a week or two later. The man performing the spell was very happy with the result.

From Frieda Lowe of NYC

From Santeria
A Spell To Enslave A Lover, Tying Them To You

Take a piece of brown paper grocery bag paper. Write the name of the person to be enslaved eight times. Write the name of the person who is to enslave them over the first name at right angles to it. Turn the paper over and write the names the same way on the other side.

Take the meat of eight snails. Crush the meat on the paper with a hammer, crushing them over the names. Add crushed coco butter over the names.
Pray:

"In the same way that a snail leaves a trail,
You will always leave a trail that I can see.
In the same way that a snail crawls,
You will always crawl back to me.
In the same way that a snail is under its shell,
You will always be under me.
In the same way that a snail is under its shell,
You will always be mine."

Wrap up the paper with the ends closed. Cut a piece of Palo Jala–Jala (Jara-Jara – Septic weed, Cassia Occidentalis or Coffee Senna, Senna Occidentalis, Ditremex.) And place this on top of the paper.

Then Pray:
"Wherever you are this will pull you back to me, and bring
you back for me alone."

Cut a piece of Palo Llamho and place on top.

Praying
For me alone.

Put this on the altar for seven days, praying for the spell each day.

Reinforcement after seven days. The wrapped paper is placed on an altar that contains:
White Wine, Pompeia perfume, Rum, Cigar smoke.
Cover this and leave it on the altar overnight, then store it away,

This spell is worked through the deities Obatala and Oshun. The Reinforcement is accomplished through Oshun.

From Irving Hochburg,
A well-known NYC Santero

A Binding Spell

This spell is done as a spell of command over a walnut that has been vivified as the brain of the person who is being commanded. The words, which are to be spoken aloud in a commanding voice, are to be projected into the mind of the person as an obsession that cannot be disobeyed.

"Thou shalt be obedient to me so long as life shall empower thee.
Thy mind shall hear my every command,
Thou shall follow them, both subtle and grand.
Thy will shall completely bend to mine,
Thou shall serve me at my request and time."

I have seen this spell given in a book as an ancient witch's spell. It is not. A witch on Long Island, who used it to get a nosey neighbor off her back, created this spell in 1968. She was very successful using it, and managed to block several other overly curious neighbors from their curiosity about members of her coven. This spell was learned by a woman married to a computer programmer, who later left her husband, moved to the west coast, and became an instant authority on witchcraft.

I tell this story only to point out that you should not believe everything you hear or read, especially tales of long hidden occult groups, mysterious spell books, or whatever suddenly coming to light. In fact, all of the various occult groups around have well known, and relatively public histories. None of these groups are much over a hundred years old.

Conch Veneries Spells

The conch veneries is often used for spells with women because of its obvious resemblance to the female pudenda. It may be baptized or anointed as a true and perfect symbol of a specific female's genitalia. Once this is done, further work on it may be accomplished, such as any of the following. These spells often rely on things put into the opening of the shell, and thus into the particular woman's genitalia.

Examples are:

#1 - The name of the man who wants to have sex with her.
#2 - The name of the man who she wants to control with her sex.
#3 - Honey, to make her sex sweet for many men, or for one man in particular. If the woman wants this done, you can also add Many People Oil (Mucha Gente) or Come-Come Oil. This is often done to make a charm for prostitutes.
#4 - Tie a string around it to close it off.
#5 - Wrap the name of the man who wants to own the woman's sex around it, and tie it in place with a thread. Put the name on a slip of paper.
#6 - Tie two of them together mouth to mouth for a homosexual relationship. (One of the conch shells is made for each woman, in her name)
#7 - Tie with a string to a man's name on a shipping tag, to prepare the woman's sex for him, or for delivery to him.
#8 - Fill the opening with red tissue paper to make the woman more promiscuous, opening herself sexually to many men, by keeping her overly sexually excited.
#9 - Fill the opening with Jasmine oil to make her sex more tranquil.
#10 - Place in it a small penis, or a penis shaped object to make it belong to someone. A doll may also be used for this kind of spell. The person who will take possession of the woman gets the doll or the completed spell.
#11 - Fill the opening with sand, and seal it with clay to make it dry up and not be used.
#12 - Fill the opening with red (Capsicum) pepper to keep her pussy hot and

eager for sexual relations. The pepper may be held in place with candle wax if desired.

#13 - Seal the opening with plaster of Paris, to close it off so that it cannot be used.

To power the spell add the exudent or lubrication of the woman's bartholin glands if she wants the spell done, or add some of his semen if a man wants the spell cast.

The Conch Veneries is the sexual conch shell, and it is very useful in all forms of sex and love magic as it is considered to be the ideal symbol of the female genitalia.

SORTILEGE
THE PRAYER AND SPELL OF THE SEVEN KNOTS

You must take a ribbon or a cord, calculating that it will be long enough to be able to make seven knots at a distance of one inch from each other, more or less.

Make the first knot in the middle of the ribbon or cord, and say in a low voice:

"With this first knot I tie up and surround the physical being of (name of person) so that he remains in a perfect encirclement, in which from this moment on, the force of my love and will is with them within that circle."

The second knot is tied a little to the right of the first, a distance of an inch, or more or less of the first knot. Tie that knot saying:

"This second knot will mix the will of (name of person) to mine with the force of steel. He will not say anything, or do anything in any manner, which will not be in conformance with my desires."

The third knot is done to the left of the first. As you tie it, say: "With this third knot I tie your love and hold it firmly to mine. You will not be able to break it, even though you may intend to do so. You will never break it, nor will you ever be able to loosen it. It is my wish that your love energy toward me shall never be weakened."

You are to place the fourth knot a little to the right of the second knot. Say very slowly, as your love is felt through the words you are saying:

"Your thought(s) will be completely held to mine, and you will never be able to remove from your mind my image, which shall follow you lovingly wherever you are and wherever you may go. My love and my desires are to be accomplished as I forcibly wish them to be now. I demand this by the forces of the secret sortilege, and by my ardent prayer that I dedicate to our Holy Saint Anthony, so he be my lawyer in what I wish, advocating for my cause with sincerity, with justice, and without bad intentions."

Upon tying the fifth knot to left of the third, you must say:

"With this fifth knot I will imprison your heart. You will not be able to love another, nor will you try in any manner to long for, seek, or to fall in love with any other person. Your heart will be entirely consecrated to my happiness, and become the receptacle of my love."

The sixth knot is done a little to the right of the fourth knot, and these words are said with it:

"Your words, your thoughts, your actions, and your desires, will always long for me from this day forward.

Know now that I will hold you accountable for this, though this well placed secret sortilege, and this knot that I do place."

The seventh knot is placed to the left of the fifth, as you softly say:

Your love is now completely mine. With this knot I will close the circle in which I enclose you. You shall now remain within the perfect encirclement, which will form this magic ribbon. With this I now surround your heart; with this I will now love your heart, with this, your entire physical being will be mixed with my own. With these seven knots of love you will be mine, and we will be one from this day forward. We now stand together for each other, and nothing, nor anyone will ever be able to break, interrupt, or harm our happiness. Those who conflict with us shall certainly be destroyed."

Notes: With the last knot finished, you now tie the two extremes of ribbon or cord, taking off, or cutting, whatever is left over for a bow or a circle. From the last knot and center ligature you will put a silver-plated head, whether it be that of a man or woman. That will serve to symbolize that two hearts, two thoughts, and the wills of two people have gone into one being, becoming one thought alone, and making one supreme will.

The person that makes this sortilege will best make it in the manner of a garter, placing this bow or ribbon, on the left arm, above the elbow during seven alternate nights. Upon getting up the following day, you are to hide it in a secret place, as a favorable sortilege toward your loves. You should also dedicate to Saint Anthony and to St. Martha a small altar, where small statues of the two Saints are standing, one next to the other.

From Papa Jim

Health And Beauty Spells

To Keep Your Youthful Look

Wash your face with the dew that collects on the grass or herbs before sunrise on the First of May. The one who does this three times, on three different but consecutive years, is supposed to maintain their youthful looks forever.

A girl living on a farm in Lancaster county Pennsylvania did this by rolling nude on the dew-laden grass before sunrise on five consecutive Maydays. The Sixth May day was raining, so she could not do this, although she rolled on the grass in the rainstorm. Most of the people who knew her agreed that she kept her youthful looks long past middle age. She was well known in the surrounding area as the girl with the eighteen-inch waist, even though she had born two children.

From M. Herr
Millersville, Pennsylvania

A Weight Loss Spell

Placing a tiny bit of camel dung in the tub when bathing is supposed to allow you to lose weight easily. My informant did not tell me where to obtain the camel dung however, so I have not tried this spell.

In a more practical light, eating a normal breakfast and having a quarter head of lettuce salad for lunch, without dressing is said to usually assist you in losing weight. Beef broth and honey water have also been recommended for losing weight. My doctor does not think well of any of these ides, so I have not tried them either. They do seem more practical than using camel dung.

The Beauty Prayer Salt Rub

This involves one person giving another a salt rub, which has the physical effect of removing dead skin cells and making the person look radiant, while the person rubbing the salt on is repeatedly praying the following ditty.

All the ugly now go away
All the beauty will now stay

Health and Healing Spells

You should check these folklore and magical health suggestions with a licensed health professional before deciding to use any of them. Like all magical remedies and spells, they are not guaranteed to work, and they may actually be physically dangerous for people.

To Stop Someone From Drinking
(I do not recommend your using either of these spells –

I place them here as an example of why you should not trust
magic spells and receipts coming from folk medicine. - DM)

Both of the spells below make the person who works them on the recipient of
the liquor dislike the person who gave them the liquor. This is even more definitely
found with the mouse spell, but it is also found with the eel spell. Therefore, the
person who works this spell should not be someone whose alienation to the recipient
of the liquor would cause permanent harm to a family relationship.

#1 - Kill a live Eel and drop two drops of blood from the head of the eel into a bottle
of the alcoholic liquor that the person likes. Bury the bottle in the earth for nine days,
and then give it to the person who is to be cured of drinking.

Their first drink from that bottle will make them violently ill, and turn them
against drinking.

#2 - Put a newborn mouse in liquor the person favors for nine days. Strain the
mouse out and give the liquor to the person.

From Joseph Lukach
In New York City

To Clean The Eyes – For Infections Of The Eyes

Take a water tumbler full of warm water and squeeze the juice of 1/8 of a
lemon into it. Use this mixture as an eyewash. This mixture is good for infections and
colds in the eyes. If it burns, add more water. Keep the lemon in the dark after
cutting it.

You must make up a new solution like the above for each use.

Lucia Grimaldi gave me this when I was having eye problems.   It was
satisfactory, and of some help, but I received some medication from my physician that
cleared the problem up in a day or two.

Strengthening The Eyes

Using a teaspoon full of Eyebright herb to a pint of water, make a tea. When
the tea has steeped, but before it is strained, add a half-teaspoon full of Boric Acid.
Bathe the eyes with this solution every day. This eyewash is slightly effective in
developing the astral vision, but not really as much as is so often claimed for
Eyebright herb tea.

A tea of Eyebright herb alone is also effective, but the above solution is usually
found to be much better than the herb alone for strengthening the eyes.

Purification With The Sun And Saturn

For Saturn, use Wild Alum root. For the Sun use a mixture of Goldenseal herb and Myrrh. These herbs may be burned as incense, although the odor is not particularly remarkable.

A tea made of these herbs, either blended together or used separately, may be used successfully as a floor wash.

Myrrh can be powdered and boiled vigorously to make a tea. The solution may be removed from the heat and the goldenseal herb added to make the tea.

From Donald Nelson

Surgical Dressings

Take one teaspoon full of Goldenseal herb, a teaspoon full of powdered Myrrh, and a half-teaspoon full of red (Cayenne) pepper to a pint of boiling water. The surgical dressings are to be soaked in this mixture, wrung out, and applied to the wound. It is an excellent treatment for both wounds and swellings. The same blend in alcohol instead of water makes an excellent liniment. The alcohol from Vodka is preferred to rubbing alcohol, but an ethyl rubbing alcohol may be used.

From Joseph Lukach in NYC

Salt Rub

An excellent Salt rub for the debilitated may be made from equal quantities of Epsom Salt and Common Salt. It is a slight abrasive to the skin, and should not be rubbed over healing wounds or burns, but this salt rub removes the misma of disease, as well as abrading and removing dead skin cells.

Ideally, the person receiving the salt rub should have it applied to them by another person. This is actually a form of body massage.

Thyroid Conditions

Sugar affects the thyroid gland. Eating avocados assists those who have problems with consuming sugar.

In some cases, the ingesting of sugar debilitates the psychic senses and causes depression. People who find this to be the case should eat an avocado each week, or even as much as eating avocados three times a week.

Bladderwrack herb tea aids in balancing the thyroid gland. It is rich in iodine. The tea is made from a teaspoon of the herb to a cup of hot water. Make the tea by the cup and don't try and keep it. A cup of the tea a day is usually an adequate dose.

Burns

The best treatment for serious burns is the application of honey to the burn. This is an old Hexenmeisters remedy.

For lesser burns, sulfur and alum may be used as a dusting powder. Mix equal quantities and dust on the burn.

From Lee Gandee
in his book, <u>Strange Experience</u>

For lesser or mild burns, urinate on the burn frequently throughout the day, using your own urine. This will remove the pain and heal the burn, allowing it to heal scar free.

From Martin Jaffrey

Sunburn

For sunburn, make up a strong batch of common beverage tea. (Lipton's tea is fine) Use two tea bags to each cup of water, instead of any lesser quantity. Make up about a gallon of this mixture, and add to a lukewarm bath. Soak in the tub for at least twenty minutes. Make up an additional quart of this mixture, allow this second batch to cool, and apply to any painful areas after the bath is finished. The person bathing should air dry from this bath as well.

From J. Hoffmann

Bust Developing Massage Lubricant

This material is used to develop the bust size of a woman who wishes to increase her breast size. She should gently apply this mixture to her breasts every day, while praying for larger and more attractive breasts.

Mix: 2 ounces of coconut Oil
¼ teaspoon of powdered cascarilla bark
I teaspoon of Palm Oil
4 ounces of Coco Butter
Rouge if desired, to suit.

Blend warm and place into an ointment jar. Allow the mixture to cool before use. Keep refrigerated, but do not freeze.

Using Bluestone (Cu S O$_4$)
In Healing And Other Magic

Bluestone, blue vitriol, or Copper Sulfate. (Cu S O$_4$ 5 H$_2$ 0) The crystal is also known as cupric sulfate. This is a toxic chemical that attacks the liver; it should not be used in magic at all. Formerly it was quite frequently used in amatory magic. It has been used magically for a number of purposes, including by prostitutes to attract customers, where a solution of bluestone in water was smeared on the inner thighs of the woman before she went out to solicit trade.

The solution was also used for degrading women, and for 'catching one's true love,' according to Regina Nicer, who worked from 1850 to 1870 in New Orleans.

Copper Sulfate is not ever recommended for use in magic for any purpose at all. It is too dangerous to use successfully in magic.

The so-called Wound Salve is made from copper sulfate that has been crystallized at the vernal equinox. The efficiency of this treatment is still a matter of some debate.

Joseph Lukach said that Bluestone is useful in the treatment of pussy infections, and Gangrene. This is to be accomplished in the following manner: A saturated solution of copper sulfate in water is made up, and a bit of the pussy bandage from the person is added to it. (Some of the puss from the wound must be on the bandage) The solution with the bandage is prayed over for the healing of the person, and then entire container is placed on the altar for seven days.

Note that the Bluestone (Copper Sulfate) is never put on the person when working this last spell.

Men's Sexual Problems

These herbal remedies are useful as a strong tea, taken daily or more often, but they are even better as tinctures, taken at a wine glass full – two ounces, each day.

Saw Palmetto Herb   -   For prostate enlargement, a weak sexual drive, Testicular problems, and Impotency. Best for prostate problems in men.

Cotton Root Herb   -   The tea is used for sexual Lassitude, and to increase sexual interest.

Damiania Herb - The tea is used for impotency, to increase the sexual drive in both men and women, and to increase the desire nature.

Muira Puama - The tea is used for Impotency, and erectile dysfunction.

Devil's Bit - Used for sexual Lassitude.

Massage Oils

Safflower oil, Almond Oil, and Cottonseed oil are all used as massage oils.

Susan Tredway recommended Strawberry oil. Of necessity, this is an artificial strawberry scent in carrier oil. She said that it was good massage oil.

Tom Hackett prefers to use coco butter as a massage medium.

For a Painful Menses

Powdered yellow Pemba is prayed over and put on the woman's bare stomach with a prayer that her menses be less painful. This must be done at every period to be effective.

One of the Homeopathic remedies for this problem are squid ink, whose tablets are started four days before the expected onset of the menses, and continued until the end of the menses. (6x potency, four tablets four times a day) After three or four periods using this treatment, the pain and discomfort of the menses usually disappears forever.

Home Protection Spells

Making Astral Snares and Traps

When they are made with intent, astral snares and traps form an obstacle to any wandering astral body. They are discouraging to the human dead, as well as being discouraging to those who are projecting from their physical bodies. Such snares and traps also are also discouraging to non-physical entities, which often find them to be not worth passing through or otherwise dealing with. There are several kinds of these snares and traps, and in practice, they may be used interchangeably, as none of them seem to be particularly specific in their nature or action.

#1 - Put into a small jar, like a baby food jar, water, black ink, pins, needles, nails and broken glass. Write the name of the person you wish to snare on a piece of paper, if known and put it into the jar. As a general snare, write the word 'everyman' on the paper. Close the jar and place it upside down by the front door.

The bottle described above may be used to trap the projecting spirit, if it is known by name. This is done placing the bottle upside down on this marked paper.

In this case, once the spirit has been caught, the paper must be burned or torn to release the wandering spirit.

#2 - Write a random assortment of lines on a piece of paper, placing circles wherever the lines cross. It should not be a grid, as the lines should be both straight and curved. The paper may be placed near an entryway or under a small rug. It acts as a spirit trap, and confuses the wandering spirit.

#3 - Put into a small jar, like a baby food jar, some black ink along with a volatile liquid, such as ether, alcohol, or chloroform. The solution should be black. Seal the bottle and place it where you desire to keep spirits away. This makes spirits lose their way. It is also a necrotic; as it causes the spirits to lose energy trying to find their way out of the fog this bottle produces around them. The fog, and leaving it weakens the spirits. It may also be used with the written spirit trap above. Place it in the center of the spirit trap. Again, the paper must be destroyed to free the spirit once it has been caught.

#4 -   A fishnet may be prepared as a spirit trap as well. Cleaning it, washing it, and praying over it will prepare the fish net for use as a spirit trap. It may then be placed under the front door rug, where it will trap spirits who attempt to enter the house.

To Protect a House or Apartment

This charm is used to protect a house or apartment against negative influences of all kinds. Take the shells of two eggs and crush them to a powder. Add some cemetery earth, and powdered patchouli herb. Add some rum into this mixture and make it into a thick paste. Place the paste into a small bottle. Now take a feather and insert it halfway into the bottle. Hold the feather in place with the drippings of wax from a candle. The feather should be firmly anchored into the bottle. You can now pray over the bottle for the protection you desire.
(EG: From all things, physical or non physical, from all forces visible or invisible.)
Tie a string around the bottle and hang it from the doorknob outside the door.

Sealing Doors or Windows

This sealing of doors or windows should be done forcefully, and spoken aloud. It is done to keep out non-physical dark forces of all kinds. The prayer may be modified, and an oil or powder may be used, as the person performing this ritual desires.

Stand before the closed window, doorway, or open passageway. Make the sign of an equal limbed cross, from top to bottom, and from left to right, while saying.

"By this sign is this entrance sealed!"

"This entrance is henceforth sealed against all undesirable and incognito entities, against all from the hosts of darkness, against all who are of negative intent, and against all who would hurt or harm. In the name of Almighty God, the creator and sustainer of the universe. Amen."

Protecting Against Evil

The following protections are in addition to the ones given in the Spiritual Workers Spell Book. See those as well, especially if there is any question of what should be done in any specific case.

The following protections are particularly effective against the force of the human dead.

#1 - To protect a home against evil.

Place a glass of water that has a few pieces of coco butter in it by the front door of the house. When someone who has evil intentions passes by the glass, the coco butter will turn dark, (brown, gray, even turn black) and may even sink in the glass. Note that this does not remove any of their evil intentions from the person.

The coco butter should be bitten off using the teeth, not cut with a knife. The coco butter in the water calms the spirit forces, especially those with destructive intent. Only small pieces of coco butter should be used. Pieces the size of a wooden match head are best.

#2 - To protect a person when visiting, sleeping, etc.

Set out a clear glass full of water in the room with a prayer that you be protected. When sleeping, put a piece of camphor in the glass, as this assists in attracting evil things to the water.

The camphor in the water vaporizes and dissipates the spirit forces, which then disappear. Many spirit forces are attracted to the odor emanating from camphor, although it takes energy from them.

Protective House Wash for a New Home

Wash out the house, from front to back with a solution made up as follows, using a new mop. Any remaining wash water should be thrown out of the back door of the house.

To a three-gallon bucket of wash water, add a mixture made as follows:

Ammonia, Florida Water, ½ teaspoon of sugar, a tea made of equal parts of Mint and Basil, a tea made of Araza con Todo, some cinnamon sticks, some sunflowers. If additional money is desired in the home, some parsley should be added to this mixture.

If the house or apartment is not new to those occupying it, a head of lettuce should be rolled through the premises first, to clean out any emotional residue the former tenants may have left there.

See my book Spiritual Cleansing for further information on this subject.

To Send Away the Spirits of the Dead

This bath is said to be very effective for removing the influence of the spirits of the dead from a person. It is to be taken before the person goes to sleep. They should either air dry or go to sleep immediately after taking it. Every opening of the body must be bathed in this bath, the mouth rinsed out, and the nostrils rinsed with the bath water.

> In a three-gallon Mop bucket, add
> Two fresh sunflowers
> Two Yellow flowers, of any kind
> Two white flowers, of any kind,
> Two red roses
> Violet Water perfume
> Mint oil
> Coconut oil
> A handful of dried Chamomile flowers
> Holy water from a church
> Rose Water
> Two handfuls of dried mint leaves
> Pompeia perfume.

Place all of the above in a crockery or glass container and cover for twenty-four hours. Then add the liquid to the bath water.

Roots In Oil

These are some of the roots used in root magic, or natural magic, which are often 'put up' in oil. The oil is believed to accept and hold the virtue of the roots. These prepared oils are then rubbed on the hands of the person using them. Through this action, the people using the oil accept the virtue of the root, placing it on themselves. These oils may also be placed in a bath; a teaspoon full of the oil to a tub bath is sufficient. The roots may be steeped in Olive Oil, any vegetable oil, cooking oil, or even Mineral Oil, as is desired by the person making up the oil, and is somewhat dependent on the purpose for which the oil is to be used.

The best-known roots that are put up in oil are the following:

HIGH JOHN THE CONQUEROR - Used for finding a job, for gambling luck, and for protection against anything.

MANDRAKE - Used to bring and hold lovers together, and for protection of the relationship from all evils.

TONKA - Used for luck and in gambling. Those wagering on sports pools especially favor this oil.

DEVILS SHOESTRING - Used as dominating oil. This oil can be used to bind an enemy.

ROSE OF JERICHO - Used for money drawing, to keep money in the house. Also use on the doors of the house, as well as on your hands, to bring money.

LOW JOHN THE CONQUEROR - Used to turn back hexes and curses. It is said to pacify your enemies.

SNAKE ROOT - Used to gain victory in court cases, and to have power over others.

INDIAN ROOT - Used for luck in gambling, especially for bingo, and luck when playing the lottery. This oil is also used to prevent the evil eye.

INDIAN TOBACCO - Contains leaf tobacco, and is often made from a crushed cigar and mineral oil. Used for court cases, and for overcoming legal entanglements.

SOME PRAYERS FROM PAPA JIM

A MONEY DRAWING PRAYER

A Daily Prayer, To Be Made Before Leaving Home In The Morning.

With the help of God, I will always have anything I need. I have my wallet blessed by God. It is open, not only to receive, but also to give to the needy. Permit me to use this money wisely. There should be no road closed to me.

If I should need something, please God, show me the way to obtain it. I have faith in your bounty.

Oh Lord, You who have the power to give, help me resolve my problems, and let me have enough money and health to satisfy my needs.

Amen.

A MONEY DRAWING PRAYER
TO BE MADE OVER A GOLD SEVEN DAY CANDLE

Holy Father thru the grace of your goodness, please help me with the money I need to get thru the day, and to better my family's life. I ask you for this small amount of money _____ in return I will offer the following to you _____.

You must light and keep burning a gold seven-day candle, in a glass container. Put nine drops of Primrose Oil in the candle each day. Light gold money drawing incense each day. Carry a holy family medal in your wallet. Make three crosses on your chest each day, with Vesta or blessing powder .

ITEMS NEEDED:

Prayer - 2 gold 7-day candles - Primrose oil - Gold money drawing incense - Holy family medal - Vesta powder

THE PRAYER OF THE GOOD PATH

I invoke the sublime influence of the Eternal Father in Heaven to obtain success in all the affairs of my life and to level all the difficulties that are in my path.

I invoke the help of the Holy Spirit so that the good stars will light my path, and drive away all of the evil shadow that may follow me.

I invoke the name of God so that my home will prosper and my purpose, and person, will receive the message of good luck sent by Divine Providence. Oh, Great Hidden Power, I implore your supreme Majesty to keep me away from danger and let my path be illuminated by the Beacon of Good Fortune.

Eternal father help me with these present difficulties that trouble me. _____ for your assistance in helping me, I will light a purple candle to you every day for 15 days.   Amen.

You are to rub each candle with Hyacinth Oil and light it, then light pure Myrrh Incense on charcoal. Once the smoke rises from the incense you are to say the prayer and make your request. You must keep burning a purple candle each day for 15 days.

ITEMS NEEDED:

One Prayer - Hyacinth Oil - Myrrh incense - Charcoal - 15 7" purple candles -

PRAYER TO THE WORKER

This is one of the most powerful prayers that a working person may pray every day. It should be prayed before going to work in the morning.

Jesus, Mary, and Joseph, when I get up, I ask for work, health, and progress. Joseph, a working man, come with me when I go to obtain my bread with the sweat of my brow. The Three Angels of Jesus come with me, and speak for me when I go to solicit work. Saint Joaquin, Saint Peter, Saint Michael, I ask also, and the Seven Creeds that I pray to as well. I ask that you help me through Jesus, Mary, and Joseph.

Oh, my God, give me bread if you think I deserve it. If not, it will be your will that decides my fate. Pardon me for my ignorance in having failed your laws.

Amen.

When you have a specific request, add this to your prayer.
St. Joseph, my request is_____ .

To honor St. Joseph you must burn a St. Joseph Candle, for each request. You should rub the candle with All Spice Oil, before lighting it. Carry his holy card in your pocket.

St. Joseph is an excellent saint for people who are looking for work, or who may need help on the job, or those who have any job related problems.

Remember that the saints must always be rewarded for the work they do. This is why candles are burned to the saints by the faithful.

THE PRAYER OF THE SEVEN (7) AFRICAN TOOLS

Jesus Christ's father Joseph was a carpenter, and so was his son, our Lord Jesus Christ. A carpenter's tools are the most significant items of his trade. Therefore, the symbols of each of the seven working tools of the seven African Powers are synonymous with our everyday lives. The seven Working Tools of the Seven African Powers are as follows:

Hold each tool as you recite these words: All Seven Saints came to my aid.
CHANGO - HAMMER: The Driving force of my love
ORULA   - SAW   Cut obstacles from my path, enforce my commands
OGUM   - CHISEL: Engrave my dreams into reality
ELEGUA - MALLET: Make my force of domination complete

OBATALA - WRENCH: Secure my need of money, so I have a full supply
YEMALLA - PLIERS: Aid me in grasping power and success in my work
OCHUN   - HATCHET: Grant me protection me against all that is evil

In the name of the Father, Son, and Holy Ghost. My heart tells me this petition is just and will be honored.
Now say your request, and make the sign of cross.

Start this prayer on a new moon. - Pray all Seven Saints each day of the week, until you have attained your heart's desire.
Pray every week. I trust in God and in our Lord, Jesus Christ, the carpenter of souls. Lord I know you will give me the strength I need. Forever and ever will I be indebted to him for his constant love and the salvation he has provided me.   Amen.

Some Miscellaneous Spells

Law Court Spells

1 -   Place a piece of paper with the petitioners name on it on top of a large
     (6" x 9") piece of cotton. On top of that put small pieces of coconut, coco butter, and sugar, all in moderate quantities. Place the name of the judge in the case on top. Fold over the cotton so that everything is inside, and carry it in your pocket to court.

2 -   Place three 'grains of Paradise' under your tongue and pray for a successful
     resolution to the problem for which you are going to court. At the hearing or trial, place the three grains of paradise on the floor, as close to the desk of the judge as possible. (Grains of Paradise are also known as Guinea peppers - Amomum Melegueta Roscoe, a plant of the ginger family.)

Traditional

3 -   A Santeria Court Spell – Before going to court light a white candle for
     Obatala and a votive candle for Ochossi, asking for a favorable outcome to the matter. Wear as much white clothing as possible when going to court.

From Irving Hochburg
A New York City Santero

Using Lava In Magic

To Stop People

Take volcanic lava that has flowed and stopped. Pray over the lava for what you wish. Place it near the person, under their desk or workspace, under their bed, or on their person.

To Expedite a Spell, Move Someone
Or Make Someone Move

Take some volcanic lava that has been expelled from the volcano, and has settled to the earth. Pray over the lava for what you want. Place this lava with a trace of the person, add it with a prayer to a spell whose effect you want hastened, or place it near the person, or where they will walk on it or otherwise contact it, to make them move.

From Elena in NYC

Spells with Indigo Blue Balls
Also Known As Anil

These are the round or often misshapen bluing balls formerly used in commercial laundries. They contain Indigo Bluing, which is the active ingredient in the blue balls. They are used to make the Blue water for Yemenja used on the altar by some Santeros. The powder of the blue balls is used to make the afloche or powder of Yemenja, which is used to bless people in the name of Yemenja.

The blue balls are also used in baths and in washes to add power, as the Indigo blue color has the ability to build the astral nature of the person, place, or thing, to which it is applied.

Indigo Blue Power Bath

Bathe each day for nine consecutive days in water in which an Indigo Blue Ball has been dissolved. In each bath pray for an increase of your astral power.

Indigo Blue Floor Wash for a New Home

Use the following as a floor wash to purify and strengthen the home after the home has been cleaned of the previous tenants vibrations.

1 Indigo Blue ball
1 cup of ammonia
1 gallon of water

This mixture is to be sprinkled on the floor, or the floor moped with it.

Using Indigo Bluing To Encourage A Pregnancy

Dissolving one blue ball in a cup of water makes indigo blue water. The water is prayed over, and then applied to the stomach of the woman who desires a child, from the navel to the pubes. Once this area is wet with the blue indigo water, the woman's abdomen stomach and pubic area is prayed over by the person who applied the blue water to the woman.

The woman receiving this treatment should be sure to copulate frequently at her most fertile times.

Clay Doll Magic

Make a doll out of ordinary children's modeling clay, with the part of the person that is to be worked on emphasized or exaggerated. As an example, the heart might be emphasized to change the person's heart in a particular way more favorable to the one doing the spell. Use a pin to indicate the nature of the problem. An ordinary pin can have a head made of clay and painted to indicate the color according to the scheme below.

Red for anger or passion
Blue for calm or contentment
Yellow for mental conditions, as mental love or madness
Black for obsessions and obsessive thoughts
Green for health

Place the pin in the doll in the area to be governed, as Black obsession in the head, Yellow mental love to the heart. Baptize the doll with seawater.

These dolls are best made at the new moon, and baptized with the degree of the sun of the native ascending. At the baptism of the doll, call for a spirit to enter into the doll to do what it is that you wish to be done with the person whom the doll represents.

"I call upon the spirit of _____ to enter into this doll to animate it and give it life, so that ___name___ may be changed ___desire for them___ in accordance with the god's desire and thereby be brought closer to his/her creator."

A Santeria Floor Wash, Used To Improve Tips

Take a large bunch of Parsley, snip it apart with scissors, while saying, "Ochun bring money" with each snip. Put into a gallon of water, soak three days, and strain. Add some honey and cinnamon oil, some rain water and some seawater. Place the water on the altar with five yellow candles, asking Oshun to bless the mixture to open up the spirit of giving in the people. Add this water to the mop water used to mop the premises.

A General Charm

For both luck and money, the Cassia nut is often worn on a string around the neck.

An 'Electric' Protective Charm

This charm is a very protective charm, as it places an 'electrical' energy through the person, which aids them in ridding themselves of all influences which either may already be on them, or which might come to them. The charm is made with five beads, strung into a necklace in the following pattern.

Coral, Jet, Amber, Jet, and Coral.

The beads are strung on a necklace string, and are made so that the center amber bead is located at the base of the trachea. It is held in place with a square knot, and left on at all times, including for bathing, sex, and sleep.

From Joseph Lukach, In NYC
At a talk on 5/16/1977

Blessing The Feet

The feet of a person may be blessed by marking the soles of the shoes with an equal limbed cross, using blessed, or consecrated white chalk. (Which may be powdered.) This is somewhat easier than blessing the bare feet with Cascarilla.

Palm oil and Cascarilla are also used to bless the hands and feet, as well as the other articulations of the body. This is done to promote grounding and stability in a person.

Lotus root powder and Orris root powder may be added to olive or almond oil and prayed over for blessing the articulations of the body for spiritual stability, or for general spiritualization. This mixture should be consecrated before use to obtain the best effects from it.

A Good Luck Bath

Boil the following together in water for an hour or more until thoroughly cooked. Let the mixture set until the water is cool. Strain out the vegetables and strain the liquid out using cheesecloth.

3 heads of lettuce
3 pounds of red Onions
3 big bulbs of Garlic
3 bunches of Parsley

Add the water to a half tub of bath water. Stir the bath water clockwise, enter into the tub with the left foot, and leave it with the right foot. Stay in the tub twenty-one minutes. Air dry after the bath, then dress in clean clothing. Take the vegetables and throw them into a river.

From Odessa in NYC

Low Spirit Charm

This charm may be used for anyone, for elevation and spiritualization. Take a chamois skin bag, put into it some Sandalwood bark and hyssop herb. Anoint the herbs with concentrated rose oil. The person receiving this charm is to pray the 23d psalm over it every day.

From Lucy Stampedos in NYC

Exorcism Spell

Go through the house room by room, censing the home with incense, from the front to the back of the house, including all closets and cupboards. Seal the windows and the doors with incense, by making three equal limbed crosses in this manner:

Make a horizontal line saying, "I cancel out the Evil." Then make a vertical line saying, "I bring down the protective light."

Once the house has been censed, go back and do all of the doors making the symbol of the pentagram, using either your hand or the incense, whichever you prefer.

This should not be used in a place where there is a person or an animal that is very sick, or near death.

From S. Khopkar,
NYC - 8/10/1977

A Mnemonic Mantra against Fear

There is no spot the Gods are not

Beneath, Around, Above,
Protecting, Guarding, Guiding Us,
Surrounding us with Love.

From Ellen Lazorisak
in Yardley PA - 1978

A Protection Spell

Mix together in equal quantities powdered Verbena and powdered Acacia. Divide the mixture into three piles. Burn the herbs on charcoal, reducing to ash, a third of the mixture at a time. As the herbs are being burned, light a candle and mediate on the subject at hand, praying for protection. When the herbs have been reduced to ash, and the candle is out, take the remaining ash and dust it around the area to be protected.

From Susan Roberts, a New York City Writer
Who received it from Victor Anderson in California

Removing the Ability to Perform Magic

The two things that have to be determined before taking any action are the source of the person's influence, and the protection of the person. The person's protection must first be removed. Then the source of the influence, the hands, eyes, mouth, feet, etc. should be covered. Once this source of influence has been covered it makes it a great deal more difficult for the person to work magic.

Ask to see the source of the person's power, and then stop it. If the means of stopping the person's power is not obvious, you may ask to have the nature of their power, as well as its source, be revealed to you.

Spells Dealing With Speech

The Myth of the Oba's Food
A Yoruba Folk Tale

One day the Oba of Ile-Ife asked his advisors while they were gathered around him in council, what food was both the best and the worst of foods. The Oba and his council all sat on the porch of the Oba's council house, all on the same level as they thought about the Oba's question. The discussed it among themselves, and debated the answer hotly.

The several advisors brought up in suggestion all kinds of foods, but the best that they could decide on was palm wine, which is both refreshing, but also leads men to undertake dangerous and foolhardy acts. The Oba smiled wisely at them, and asked them to think about his question overnight. He added that he would expect a different answer in the morning. Then he seriously said that if they were to advise him, they certainly had to be able to answer questions that were too difficult for him to comprehend. The advisors all met that night, pondering the question far into the night. Although many foods were considered, none of them could come up with a better answer than palm wine.

In the morning the Oba met with his advisors, who noticed that there were now mats in front of the porch of the Oba's council house. The Oba told his advisors, who were the head men of the families of Ile-Ifa, that they could not come up on the porch until they had answered his question. The advisors all spoke one at a time, from the most senior to the most junior. They all assured the Oba that palm wine was both the best and the worse of all foods. Each of them presented the reasons that they had proposed, and all of them gave good reasons for their decision that palm wine was both the best and the worst of all foods.

The Oba heard all them out. Then he said that none of them had the correct answer. The Oba explained to the advisors that the tongue was both the best and the worst of foods. He pointed to one of his praise singers, and stated that the tongue flatters, and it communicates good tidings, he pointed to one of his slave girls, saying that the tongue gives pleasure and speaks words of love and passion. He pointed to one of his messengers, and said that the tongue gives news and carries messages from far away.

Then he pointed to the earth and said that the tongue also lies, slanders, and insults. He pointed to the sky and said that the tongue gives praise to the Orisha, and to creator. Then he finished by saying that indeed the tongue is always the very best and the very worst of all foods. The men who were the advisors to the Oba applauded his great wisdom. And they decided that from then on, they would make their place on the mats in front of the Oba's porch. And this is why the advisors of the Oba of Ile-Ife sit on mats in front of the Oba's porch, instead of on the veranda, as they do in Oshobo, Igbo, Kosso, and in many of the other cities of Yorubaland.

The Magic of the Beef Tongue

To keep someone from speaking badly of you. - Write the person's name on a piece of paper. Slit the beef tongue down the center. Put the person's name into the tongue, and cover it with honey. The person will change their speech toward you.

To keep a judge from convicting. - Write the judge's name on a piece of paper. Slit the beef tongue down the center. Put the judges name into the tongue, and roll the tongue up. Tie the rolled tongue with black thread. Put the tongue into the freezer. This spell may also be used to control the tongue of the one whose name you have written and placed inside the tongue.

To make someone speak with a 'Hot Tongue.' - Slit the beef tongue down the center and insert the name of the person you are working against. Add 9 peppercorns, and 3 garlic cloves to the name. Sew three crosses 'X X X' over the slit in the tongue, closing it. Heat the tongue with hot peppers, needles, pins. The tongue should be heated whenever you want the person to speak with a hot tongue. They will speak angrily, and often explosively, regardless of whom they happen to be speaking with at the time. If desired the tongue may be kept in the refrigerator or even frozen between uses.

To make someone talk. - Baptize the tongue to make it the tongue of the person, and then always call the tongue by the name of the person. Slit the beef tongue down the center and insert the name of the person you are working against. Add a drop of mercury, and between one and three parrot feathers. Pray over the tongue, calling the tongue by the name of the person, that they shall now talk convincingly to whomever you wish to have them speak to.

For someone to speak honestly. - Take a tongue; baptize it in the name of the person who is to speak honestly. Address the tongue by the person's name. Now light a white candle to God, (Or to St. Michael, Our Lady of Mercy, or Obatala) asking them to make the person speak the truth in the matter that concerns you.

To Make Someone Talk Indiscreetly

Tie together: three parrot feathers, a slip of paper with the person's name on it, a tie to them, a photograph, a hair, or something of that kind. Place this assemblage in a bottle with a drop or two of mercury. The parrot feathers should protrude from the bottle, and other things can protrude as well. Pray over this that the person talk indiscreetly, telling everything (of the subject you wish them to speak of) and answer all questions directed to them concerning that subject fully and truthfully.

To Make Someone Speak

Take a small clear glass bottle; add a drop or two of mercury. Take a purple candle, to symbolize the person's protection, and a yellow candle to symbolize their mind. Light the candles verbally identifying them (Speak out loud). Pray to the mercury, saying that the person will not tell you what you need to know, explaining the case at issue. Once you have explained it, identifying why you need to know what they know, snuff out the purple candle, removing all of their protection.

Add about as much Full Moon seawater to the bottle as there is mercury in it. Only a bit of mercury is enough. Now pray again stating firmly that now the person will tell you what you need to know. Allow the yellow candle to burn out.

When the seawater in the small bottle evaporates, the person will speak to you fully and freely at your request. Once they do, keep pushing them for all of the details you may need to know concerning the matter. This spell is quite effective for one interview, but it does not open the person to permanent communications on the subject.

To Silence An Attorney Or A Speaker Opposed To You

Have them walk in a powder made of Raspa-lengua (Cosearia Hirsuta), Cascarilla (made from eggshells), Cinnamon, and white sugar. This spell locks the tongue of the person it is used against.

To Keep Someone From Talking

To the person, when in sight of them, or to their photograph or trace, say:
"Sealed thou art and sealed shall be
From now until I set the free.
Discretion sits upon thy lip
And will not let the wrong words slip. "

Some Home And Finance Spells

PREFACE

A friend recently showed me an article in the newspaper saying that all problems of domestic conflict could be greatly eased, if not solved, simply by increasing the household income. I actually doubt that, but I do know that with the home foreclosure rate jumping, many firms laying off workers, both emotional stress and finance are certainly major concerns for a great many people.

It is to try and assist those with financial and domestic difficulties that I have added these spells. I hope that people find them of use alleviating their trials.

These spells have all worked for me and for most of the people I have given them to. Try using them with the attitude that they will work for you as well. By always keeping a positive attitude, you will always be more successful in your efforts.

I must note here that this is not a textbook of magic. It is only a report of several spells that a person might find useful in clearing the area of their home and in stabilizing or improving their financial condition, and attempting to maintain their lifestyle. These spells are designed for individuals desiring to help themselves, they are not intended for the experienced magician, who will probably find grievous fault with them, as they seem to do with most of my books.

If you have any serious domestic or personal problems of a non-physical nature, see my book Spiritual Cleansing, which is a manual of non-physical first aid for those people who may find themselves in those difficulties. You may also see A Spiritual Workers Spell Book, which contains a number of remedies for many other of life's difficulties.

Draja Mickaharic

Calming And Refreshing The Home

Please - Use this simple spell first, as it will make using the other spells easier for you. I consider this to be a fundamental spell for insuring that you live in a peaceful and prosperous home.

I believe that a home should be a place of peace and calm, a place of refuge for you and your family. Unfortunately, this is always not the case. Argument and tension occasionally occur in the most loving home, as well as in the tightest bonded of families. The following 'spell,' will materially aid you in restoring peace and calm to an otherwise troubled home. Doing this frequently, say at least once a month, will insure that your home maintains a peaceful and calm vibration, and that any emotional disturbances that may occur are minimized.

If you have young children in your home, you might wish to use this spell once a week, as it will soften the often very nervous energy that healthy young children naturally display.

Of course, should there be any kind of emotional upset in the home, you will find that performing the following spell will often soften the disturbance in the home resulting from emotional upset.

I will add that for many years I used this 'spell,' at least once a month in my own home. The friend with whom I now live does the same. He told me he has also been doing this same spell for many years.

I call this a spell, but it is actually a kind of mechanical action, as this is actually a form of what is known as natural magic. The effects of this spell have nothing to do with any non-physical influence, except that resulting from the procedure itself. It is the mechanical action of the procedure itself that results in the change in the feeling, vibration, or atmosphere of the home.

Take a half-teaspoon of powdered cinnamon and add it to a half pot of water.

Place this on the fire and allow the cinnamon and water mixture to boil vigorously for about an hour or possibly even longer. As it boils, you will probably have to add additional water. You must be careful to not allow the water to boil off and the pan to run dry!

The first time you do this spell, you may wish to add an additional half-teaspoon of cinnamon. This will allow the full odor of the boiling cinnamon to thoroughly permeate your home.

The goal of this spell, or process, is to allow the odor of boiling cinnamon to permeate your whole house, so you should be certain to open all of the rooms and interior doors as the cinnamon boils.

Take at least an hour to boil this cinnamon water, especially the first time you do it. I prefer to allow the cinnamon water to boil for an hour every time I do this, as it encourages the scent and the vibration of cinnamon to permeate through out my living space.

That's really all there is to it! Simple isn't it? That's all the more reason to do this frequently. It will make your home a place of peace and rest for your family.

The only possible modification of this spell I have ever heard of is to use an iron pot to boil the water and cinnamon in. While using an iron pot is supposed to make the spell stronger, I have never noticed any great improvement in the effect. I have used a copper bottomed Revere ware stainless steel saucepan for many years. That may very well count as an iron pot with this spell.

Keeping Unwanted People
Away From Your Home

There are several kinds of unwanted visitors who may wish to come to your home for many various reasons. People you dislike are but one example. Bill collectors, tax assessors, and the police are another class of those people you might wish to keep away. We will begin with a few simple precautions to keep away those whose name you do not know.

The Police

Obviously, the best way to keep the police away from your home is to do nothing that would give them a reason to visit. Of course, if you should be faced with an eviction or a foreclosure proceeding, you may not have that option, as police usually accompany the people who serve these papers, and enforce the vacating of property.

One of the classical methods of keeping the police away from you home is to make an equal limbed cross on the back (inside) of your front door using coco butter.

This is not a hundred percent sure-fire method, but it does seem to work often enough to maintain its reputation as a useful spell.

I would advise doing this as a first line of defense should you believe you might have problems with the law, finance companies, or collection agencies. I would also use this spell if anyone else in authority might be threatening you or your home. This might include people such as building inspectors, property tax investigators, unwanted missionaries, and so forth. You can purchase coco butter at most drugstores. Only a light equal limbed cross about a foot in each direction is needed, it is not necessary to make a very large or prominent mark on your door. The mark need not even be visible to the casual visitor.

According to Ms. Catherine Yronwode, gaining warning of police interest was once accomplished by fixing Indian head pennies to the door, the Indian facing out. These pennies are rather rare today, and often expensive. A friend of mine who was briefly involved in a dubious if not illegal gambling activity put a small picture of an Indian over his front door. The picture my friend used was cut from one of those sold as holy cards in occult stores. He only used the head of the Indian, and while it looked a bit odd glued over his front door, he said that he never had problems with the police while it was there. I know that when he removed the Indian's picture, he received a summons for an overdue parking ticket within a day or two. That event was the cause of some merriment for many of his friends.

Foiling Visits From
Finance Companies And Collection Agencies

This is a spell I have not used, but a friend I trust said that it worked for her, so I will pass it on in hopes that it will work for you, should you ever need to use it.

"When bill collectors threaten to come to your door, or finance companies threaten to repossess your furniture or appliances, roll up a dollar bill, seal it with a piece of tape, and place it at the foot of the hinge side of your door, saying that this is to pay them, naming the company, what they want. Naturally, should you see them come to your door, you should not open the door to them. In a short time they will usually stop troubling you."

It might not be obvious, but you should do this as soon as you suspect that you might be in trouble with these people. You should not wait until they are knocking at your door. When that happens, it's too late for any magic you might do to work for you.

A Broom Corn Spell To Keep People Away

I actually learned this spell from my mother when I was a schoolboy. She used it to keep people from visiting us when either she or my grandmother was in a black mood, or whenever someone in the house was sick. Take two straws plucked from the broom you sweep the floor of your house with. Make an X or cross of them and place them behind your front door, or lay them on the floor behind your front door. Then put a tiny dab of salt on the floor behind the door. In this case only a very few grains of salt are required. Be stingy with the salt, three or four grains are enough.

Spells to Keep People Away
When You Know The Person's Name

I have used this spell many times, and found very few people who ever managed to cross my doorway after I used it against them. The spell only requires that you have someplace to put the saucer and glass used in the spell on the opening side of your door. If you have to set it on the floor, you must be very careful of the spell when you open the door or let people into your home. I highly recommend this spell, as it has never failed me.

Write the name of the person who is to be kept away from your home on a piece of scrap paper, using a lead pencil. Place the paper in a small glass, like a juice glass, and fill the glass about two thirds full of water, wetting the paper. Now place a saucer on top of the glass and invert the glass. The glass with water in it will now be upside down on the saucer. Unless there is some problem, such as a chip in the glass, the water will not leak out. Place the saucer with the upside down glass at the opening side of your doorway, the side opposite the hinge. The person whose name is in the glass will decide to no longer visit you.

A Spell To Discourage Visitors
To Your Home

This spell is useful if you have someone who is sick and needs constant attendance. In this event you may not have time to answer the door and attend to those people who seem to call only to want to annoy you or sell you something. This spell will not keep everyone away, but if you are trying to discourage visitors generally, or if you have one person you wish to discourage, this spell is useful in addition to whatever else you might be doing toward that cause.

Take several tablespoons of four thieves vinegar and sprinkle them on the front steps of your home. If you wish, you can dilute the vinegar half and half with water and sprinkle on your steps and the sidewalk in front of your home.

I have not found this spell to discourage those people who are 'on a mission,' and believe they must see you, but it does seem to discourage many other random and generally unwelcome visitors. I think it's worth a try to use whenever you wish to discourage visitors, or slow down the traffic to your home.

Protecting Your Job

The following spells are good for those people who have difficulty at their job, particularly those who are at risk for being laid off, or discharged because of a company merger or downsizing. These are primarily protection spells, more useful in maintaining and holding a position than in gaining one. However they are also good spells to use when you are already employed and are attempting to win a promotion to a better position.

White Eggshell Spells

Finely powdered white eggshell, like four thieves vinegar, is one of the more useful magical ingredients. The eggshell is a symbol of purity, honesty, virtue, and good intentions. To make this useful item, set aside several white eggshells, after peeling out their internal membrane. Allow the shells to dry thoroughly. Once they are dry, crush the eggshells into a fine powder. The finer the powder the eggshells are crushed into the better the powder will work. Bottle the white powder in a small well-stoppered bottle, and keep it dry.

Displaying Innocence

To display to others that you are innocent of anything of which you might be accused, place a small pinch of the white eggshell powder in your hair. This will usually stop suspicion and accusations of most kinds, unless the accusation is backed by some kind of solid evidence. A pinch of the white powder, much less than an eighth of a teaspoon is all that you will need. Using too much will show, often making you look rather clownish.

Naturally, if there is solid evidence of your guilt in the matter, you will probably have to face some kind of charges. However, if there are only suspicions of your guilt, you will usually be exonerated.

You should begin this process of placing a pinch of the eggshell powder in your hair as soon as you beleive there might be any suspicion directed to you. Continue placing a small pinch of the eggshell in your hair until the matter is closed. This often requires your doing this spell each day for several weeks.

Should you believe people are talking about you and making veiled accusations or threats, you might begin using this spell as soon as you have these suspicions. Doing so often nips these accusations in the bud, as people who know you will not believe that you could be guilty of such things.

For Gaining Stability In Your Employment

When you concerned about your employment, as in being concerned that your position may be eliminated through downsizing, that your firm may be sold, or that other difficulties are in sight, this is a spell to immediately consider using. If you suspect that something of this nature might be in the works, or of you have been feeling opposition to you at your workplace, you might prepare the material to have it ready to use if the situation should change, or as often happens, begins to turn against you.

Take about a quarter cup of horse corn, that dry solid corn often found in bird feeders, and available from almost all animal and pet food merchants. Crush the corn; in some cases a hammer may be useful for this. Then roast the corn in your oven until at least some of the grains display an even brown color. Allow the corn to cool. Then mix it with the white eggshell powder in the ratio of about two tablespoons of corn to a half teaspoon of the white eggshell powder. The finished compound should be kept in a sealed bottle, where it will be kept free of contaminants.

To use this corn for your benefit, sprinkle about a quarter teaspoon to a half a teaspoon full of the mixture on the ground in your work area. It is not necessary to have a large visible presence of this mixture, as a moderately obscure trace will do as well. If it only looks like a slightly dirty floor, you have attained your goal.

As most office floors are cleaned every day, you will have to repeat the sprinkling of this material each day. If you work in a place where the floors are cleaned only every week, such as an automobile garage or a mechanical workshop, you will have to re sprinkle some of the material each time the floors are cleaned. The object is to keep a slight amount of this mixture on the floor under your feet.

The result of this practice is similar to that of placing the powdered eggshell in your hair, in that the people you work with will look at you as someone who belongs in that position, and who does good work there. For the most part, these people will not wish to see you leave the employment you enjoy.

Walking In Virtue

Should you be suspected of using your sexuality improperly at work, you should pray over some of the white eggshell powder that you project an image of virtue, and place a pinch of it in each shoe. This spell should accompany placing a pinch of eggshell powder in your hair. The combination will make it difficult for people to believe you misuse your sexuality.

This spell is also useful to encourage a girl to maintain her virtue. For this use, the white powder should be added to her shoes every day beginning with the day of her first menstrual period. All parents know this is often a struggle between nature and social rules, and the struggle must be continued for a good long while to be effective.

Overcoming Envy, Jealousy, And Gossip

I have written about this technique several times, but I will place it here again, for the benefit of those who may not be familiar with it. I consider this spell to be the primary office workers protection, although it is also very useful in protecting workers in any other field.

Jealousy and gossip are one of the trials of working in an office. Many people seem to have nothing else to do but talk about others. Naturally, because these are usually very negative people, their words are usually critical and often destructive. While their negativity will fall back on them in time, this is not sufficient compensation for those who are the victims of these vicious negative people. It is necessary to guard against these people, and prevent their sly and cutting words from harming anyone who might become the attention of their nasty wagging tongues.

Take a quarter teaspoon of cinnamon and add it to about three or four heaping tablespoons of talcum powder. Mix this well, so the cinnamon color is lost in the talcum powder, or at least nearly lost. This is the mixture you will use, and it should be kept in a closed and labeled bottle in your bathroom or on your dresser.

As you dress for work each day, take a SMALL amount of this mixture on a fingertip and place it on your sternum. For men, this is your breastbone, for women, this is in the cleavage between your breasts. You must be frugal with this powder; as much as would be the size of a match head is quite enough. If you over use this powder you will quite possibly end up smelling like a candy bar. This is not always a good odor to have around you in the office.

The daily use of this product will discourage people gossiping about you, and it will also reduce the harmful effects of any thoughts or words of envy and jealousy that may be directed at you. I highly recommend doing this, as it can also prevent low-level malochia from affecting you.

Some Spells For Financial Improvement

In my <u>Spiritual Workers Spell Book</u>,[1] I give a number of spells for improving a person's finances. All of the spells given there, with the one exception given below, are different from the spells I give here. The spell I am repeating is one that I have often used myself, and have found to always be productive of increased income, so long as the money in the house was being well managed. If you believe you are a wastrel or one who has no respect for money, I advise you not to use it. In that case the spell may actually be harmful to you.

Please note that this spell is only useful for improving the finances of a home, it does not enhance the finances of one particular person. Furthermore, you must be unconcerned as how the money comes to you. Please do not decide that it may only come from winning the lottery, a large pay raise, or something similar. Doing so will actually limit the potential inflow of money coming to you from performing this spell.

As an example of this, one time, when I was particularly lacking funds, I found sixty dollars in a small coin purse in the street, with no address or other indication of where it might have come from. I hardly could have expected this as an answer to my prayer.

Dried Bean Household Money Spell

Take about a quarter cup each of dried black beans, dried chickpeas, and dried corn or wheat. Mix them together well, and make up four packets of the mixture, placing the mixture in plain white paper, or white cloth, packets. Place one of the packets in each of the four corners of the main room of the house. Then place three shiny new pennies on top of each of the four packets.

Leave the packets in place for some time, six months to a year is about right. Don't be in a hurry, and don't restrict your economic evolution by deciding the money must come from a raise at work, winning the lottery, or some other source. If you are willing to let God provide, God will always do so. Over the time the packets are in place the money coming into the household will increase. This will be especially true if the money coming into the household is being well managed.

---

[1] Published by Xlibris, Inc Philadelphia, PA in 2002   To purchase a copy call 1 - 888 - 795 – 4274 Or on the internet at Xlibris.com or Amazon .com

Gaining Money Through Fumigation

These fumigation spells will not be useful for you if you have asthma, COPD, or any other breathing difficulty. If you are afflicted with any of these physical conditions, you should not ever even try to fumigate yourself, or to use incense for any other purpose, as doing so could be physically harmful to you.

Please take this warning seriously. I have a good friend who suffers from this breathing difficulty. He can no longer use many magical techniques because the incense fumes actually cause him physical harm.

Fumigating Yourself

There are all kinds of reasons for fumigating yourself. There is also a big reason not to try and do so. If you have breathing difficulties of any kind, you must avoid fumigating yourself, as the fumes could seriously aggravate your physical condition. That being said, if you are physically healthy enough to fumigate yourself, this is how you may proceed to successfully do so.

You should begin with a wooden chair that is reasonably comfortable and has no armrests. The incense burner, from which the fumes originate, will be placed approximately under the center of this chair. This can be a small tin can turned upside down with a charcoal on it. You will also need a sheet with which to wrap yourself. And of course you will need the incense you wish to use to fumigate yourself.

Disrobe to the skin, as you wish to fumigate yourself, not your clothing. Light a charcoal on the incense burner, and wait until it is hot all over, as shown by the reddish glow. Then add the incense to the top of the hot charcoal. Wait until the fumes begin to rise. You are now ready for your fumigation.

Sit in the chair, and wrap yourself with the sheet, so that the bulk of the fumes coming from underneath the chair will come in contact with your body. Now just relax and remain seated until there are no more fumes. Be sure and stay seated for at least a few minutes after the fumes cease. Be patient, take your time, and allow the vibration of the incense to permeate your aura. Trying to rush these things won't work.

Once the incense has been out for a while and all the fumes are gone, get up and get dressed. Your self-fumigation is finished.

That's all very well you may say, but what incense should I use? Here's a short list:

> For finances, use either Cinnamon or Nutmeg.
> For protection, use either Cloves or Cardamom.
> For spiritual growth, use Frankincense or Benzoin.

For improving your psychic vision or intuition, use Myrrh.
To improve your relationships, use Palm Resin or Copal.

If you wish you can fumigate yourself with prepared incenses from occult manufacturers or spiritual supply stores. Please examine these carefully before purchasing or using them, as many of these incenses are nothing but coloring and perfume in a powdered wood base. These 'perfume incenses,' will not usually do very much for you at all.

There are a few (Unfortunately, Very Few) legitimate manufacturers of useful and accurately made magical supplies such as incense, oils, baths, and other things. I do not recommend any of these manufacturers because I have found that even the longest established businesses seem to suddenly go out of` business. Look around, check your yellow pages, surf the Internet, and see if you can find someone that looks good to you. If all of their web pages are catalogue items, and none of them give health warnings for specific products, they may not be either helpful or legitimate. The better manufacturers have pages full of all kinds of information for those who work with various magical practices. These are the people who deserve your business and support.

I have found some spiritual supplies on sale at Ebay, and while I have nothing against that form of retailing, I do not think that it is the best place to purchase occult products or magical supplies. If there is an occult or spiritual supplies store in your town, visit the place, see what you think of the store, their stock, and the people who run the place. If you like the store, and the people seem competent, give them your business. If not, move on to the Internet.

Spiritual Baths For Financial Improvement

In my book Spiritual Cleansing[2], I mentioned that cinnamon could be used in a bath to gain financial improvement. Two baths specifically designed for financial improvement are given in that book. One of them is given later on.

I must also mention that one of the reasons people may feel they are blocked financially is they are carrying around a lot of emotional and mental residue as psychic garbage in their non-physical body, or aura. This kind of psychic garbage is what the famous psychoanalyst Dr. Willhelm Reich referred to as DOR, or Dead Orgone Residue. This kind of psychic garbage must always be removed before the blocked person can make any further progress with their life. Unfortunately, many people carry this residue with them all of their lives. The residue is accumulated over the course of time. It originates in the course of a person's normal daily life, and is not

---

[2] A second edition was published in 2003 by Red Wheel – Weiser. It is available in bookstores and on the Internet at the Red Wheel Weiser website. This book is also sold by Amazon.com and many other Internet bookstores.

something sent to them from another person as evil thoughts, negativity, or a curse.

As it takes a person a great deal of time to accumulate the psychic clutter that blocks their life, it is not usually necessary that a person clean this psychic garbage off them more frequently than once a year. As the individual usually feels better after a cleansing bath there is a tendency for some people to repeat these cleansing baths more often than is absolutely necessary. Over frequent spiritual cleansing may prove to be as detrimental to a person as never cleaning their psychic garbage off at all. Being too psychically clean may often tend to leave the individual open to unwanted and random psychic influences. It may also possibly leave them open to being psychically manipulated by others. This is why I recommend only an annual cleansing bath.

I have found that one cleansing bath a year is usually sufficient for most people. If you believe you need more frequent cleansing baths, I suggest you consult a spiritual practitioner. If you are correct in your assessment, there may actually be another non-physical problem you are faced with.

It might not be necessary to mention this, but before you take any spiritual bath you should take a bath to wash clean your physical body. The purpose of any spiritual bath is to clean your non-physical body, or your aura. This is best accomplished once your physical body has been cleaned.

A Cleansing Bath

This is the cleansing bath recommended by Dr. Willhelm Reich. I had not known this when I originally wrote Spiritual Cleansing, as I learned about this bath from another spiritual practitioner in New York City. A reader wrote and told me that Dr. Reich had recommended this bath to his patients for the purpose of removing what he called DOR, or Dead Orgone Residue.

Take a cup full of salt and a cup full of baking soda. Mix them together, and add them to a tub of water. Stir the tub, so the mixture dissolves in the water. Soak in the bath water for at least ten or fifteen minutes. Then air dry to keep the cleansing vibration around you.

A Cinnamon Bath For
Financial Improvement

Bring to a boil a cup or two of water and a half-teaspoon of powdered cinnamon. Once the mixture is boiling vigorously, turn off the heat and allow it to cool. Add the mixture to a tub full of warm water and bathe in it for about six to eight minutes. While you are in the tub, pray sincerely for an increase in your financial condition. When you have finished bathing, leave the tub and air dry. The object of air-drying after any bath is to keep the vibration of the bath you have just taken around you.

Relationship Spells

No relationship goes through its course without hitting some rough spots. The question is always whether or not these rough spots will destroy or strengthen the relationship. Either may be the actual result of a time of troubles between a husband and wife. In some cases, rough spots can do a great deal to help a tottering relationship, because traveling over them requites the two people concerned to openly talk about things they may not have wanted to talk about before. It is often the forcing of the two partners in the relationship to talk that opens things out for them in their relationship, making their relationship stronger.

Occasionally burning allspice as an incense on a charcoal in the home can assist in promoting conversation and in clearing the air. While this is not a sure fire curative for couples that have difficulty communicating, it can often assist in bringing out for discussion the kind of petty difficulties people face in their day-to-day relationships. It might be worth trying if you and your spouse have difficulty talking things over with each other.

Unlike many other spices used for spiritual purposes, I have found no benefit from using allspice as a bath or in any other way than as incense. Even here, its benefit is only revealed in some cases. It is hardly a curative of wide effect in cases where communication is difficult. However, I beleive it is always worth trying.

The Prime Remedy

The prime remedy to apply whenever there is any kind of tension in the home, regardless of its origin, is the one given in chapter one. Allowing the scent of cinnamon to permeate the home will usually solve a great number of problems, especially easing problems dealing with relationships, finance, and children. I cannot recommend this solution often enough. Simple as it is, the boiling of cinnamon in a home has had remarkable results in bringing couples and families together, as well as in calming the home and releasing emotional tensions between the husband and wife.

Gardenia Perfume

Gardenia flowers and Gardenia perfume can assist in easing tension in the marriage. Using a little gardenia perfume or essential oil in a floor wash can assist in strengthening weak and failing relationships. Should you fear infidelity, mopping the floor with gardenia scented floor wash every week will be of assistance in reminding a possibly roving mate where their primary loyalties should lie. Make their home coming warm and affectionate, and your partner will spend less time away from home.

On this subject, I will add that panicking about a roving mate, of either sex, is the worst thing you can do, as it reveals your own feelings of low self worth. Most strongly sexed partners, of either sex, will stray in their marital relationship once or twice. If the aggrieved partner is sure of their own worth and value, and has been holding up their end of the marital partnership, there is no reason to fear the destruction of the relationship from an incident of infidelity. It is not who the partner has sex with that matters, it is whom they come home to that maintains the relationship.

I realize this is not the viewpoint most approved by society, but it is a practical and pragmatic one. Women who are overly concerned about the possibility of their husband's cheating on them are usually the kind of women the man should have divorced years ago, or better, never have married in the first place. These women are sub consciously convinced of their own low self worth, and they have no value in their own eyes. Such women make poor wives, and even worse companions over the long and often rocky path of a lifetime.

Improving Your Sex Life

It is a fact that 80% of American women wear the wrong sized brassiere. 60% of American women continually wear the wrong shoe size. If women do not know their own clothing sizes, what makes anyone believe they actually know anything at all about the more intimate details of their life?

In the course of my active practice in New York, I have had many women tell me their mother told them their husbands would explain sex to them when they were married. Some women, supposedly from good families, even had their mother tell them that good girls did not ever concern themselves about such things as sex. These are prescriptions that aim a woman directly for failure in their married life.

Please do not believe that I think men are any better informed about the details of the sexual life.

However, It is vitally important for a successful marriage that both members of the couple take an active interest in learning about, and exploring, the sexual side of their relationship. This is best accomplished together, using some of the vast quantity of printed literature, videotapes, and other material that is available today. Once both members of the relationship have a better idea of what is expected of them sexually, as the result of frequent mutually involved conversations, there is bound to be more communication concerning their sexual life. This is something that can only improve the marital relationship.

God intended the sexual relationship between human beings to be pleasurable. In fact, many spiritual teachers believe and teach that God gave two gifts to mankind to ease their difficult life on the earth. These gifts were laughter and orgasm. Humans should do whatever they can to enjoy both of these divine gifts as frequently as it is possible for them to do so.

Sexual Lubricants

One of the many problems found in human sexual relations is dryness of the female genital area, which many women seem to believe cannot be helped. When natural vaginal lubrication fails, there may be a medical problem, and a physician should be consulted. However, there are numerous lubricants available that can be used to ease this difficulty. If you wish to have a happy married life, you must be willing to take advantage of them!

Talk to a pharmacist and have them explain the details of the various sexual lubricants available. There are certainly a wide variety of these lubricants to choose from. One of these commercial sexual lubricants is bound to be the ideal lubricant for you. No one need put up with painful intercourse caused by dry female sexual organs.

Glycerin As A Sexual Lubricant

Glycerin, which is available in any drug store, when lightly applied to the female sexual organs, has a warming effect. Most people find this effect stimulating, arousing, and quite pleasant. Some people find it unpleasant and discomfiting. If you decide to try using glycerin, use a very small amount at first and see whether you enjoy it or not. If you find using glycerin in this way to be uncomfortable, it will easily wash off with soap and water.

Isopropyl Myristate

According to a chemist I know, the natural human skin and sexual lubricant is a chemical known as Isopropyl Myristate. I do not fully beleive this, but it sounds like it might be at least partly true. A client who was a salesman for a chemical company gave me a gallon of the substance for use as bath oil. I found it to be the best bath oil I have ever used, but I have no idea where you could purchase the substance today. Nonetheless I put this out there if you should be fortunate enough to find some. Supposedly it is an excellent sexual lubricant as well. I must admit that I have not tried it for that purpose.

Love Spells

I consider love spells a waste of time, as while you may gain the temporary adoration of your beloved, I will guarantee you, that after three years being intimate with them, you will be more or less finished with them. This is because human relationships are designed by Mother Nature to maintain their intensity for only about three years. After that, the passion of love dims, and the reality of having to get along with, and live with someone as a friend as well as a lover kicks in.

When you use a love spell to have someone fall in love with you, you are short-circuiting the procedure, even if your love spell works. If there is no reciprocation at all felt from the beloved to you, your love spell won't work anyway.
Sorry about that.

If, despite all this, you still want to do a love spell, you can find books full of them in the public libraries. Pick any one of these love spells you like. As was once mentioned by the famous folklorist C. G. Leland, "Love spells are the most difficult of all spells to cast, and they are the least likely to ever be successful."

As I said before, Sorry about that.

Sex Spells

On the other hand, the first commandment given by God to humankind was to be fruitful and multiply. God spoke this to Adam and Eve as he chased them out of the Garden of Eden. It should be obvious to everyone that God wants people to have sexual intercourse. In the eyes of our creator, as well as in the eyes of Mother Nature, chastity is the only real sexual perversion. Sexual intercourse is a part of the divine plan for life on the earth. Thus a spell asking that you find someone to have sex with is more often answered than a spell asking that a specific person fall in love with you.

Red Candle Sex Spell

Take a red candle, a small red birthday candle will do, and feverently pray as you light it that you find someone to have sex with. Continue to pray as the candle burns. Once the candle burns out, you should immediately go out and try to find someone to have sex with.

God will always assist you in finding a lover, but it is quite unlikely that one will be delivered to your door. You have to look for someone, and you have to be open to being pleasant to them and actively courting the person. Don't expect a lover to fall into your arms. You will have to do some of the work to get them there.

This procedure is completely in accord with the old Arabian proverb, 'Trust in God, but tether your camel first.' Whenever you pray, and whatever you pray for, God may provide an opportunity for you, but you have to do the work to make that opportunity manifest for you on this earth. God is always willing to be of assistance but it is the people asking God for assistance who must do what is necessary to make the opportunity God provides' bear fruit, and materialize physically on the earth.

Another saying worth repeating here is that a woman can always find someone to have sex with. It may not be the person they first wished to have sex with, but she can always find some one willing to have sex with her. For a man the situation is somewhat different. A man can usually find someone to have sex with, but he must be prepared for rejection, and he must do his best to present an image that will attract a woman. A man must realize that he has more work to do in this regard than a woman.

Finding A Mate

Finding a mate is a great deal different from finding a casual sexual encounter. When you believe you are ready to find a mate, you must first decide exactly what kind of husband or wife you desire. A cute nymphomaniac whose father owns a liquor store may be a humorous reply to this question for a man, but it is not nearly an adequate description of what you really want to have as a potential mate.

You should start with the obvious, knowing your physical preferences, as you have learned them from dating a number of women. Think about these first, then write them down, being absolutely honest with yourself.

An Example Of Preferences

I am looking for a blue eyed blond woman at least five feet three and no taller than five eight, who weighs between a hundred and a hundred twenty pounds. She must have at least a full A cup breast size, but not a breast cup size larger than a full B. She should either have long hair or be willing to keep her hair long. She should have at least a high school education, be fluent in English and a native English speaker.

Thus we have the beginning of the description of the woman the man is searching for. It is only the beginning, as once the description has been written out, the man should read and revise this description every night for at least a month until he finally has the description of his perfect woman, who will become his perfect wife.

A woman should write the same thing, describing on paper her perfect man, her perfect husband. Both men and women must understand that you cannot get something if you don't know what it is you really want. Once you have firmly settled on what you want, the universe will then begin to manifest it for you. Of course, if you change your mind in midstream, you will have to go back to square one and begin all over again

No, it's not really that easy, but it almost is. There is one more very big consideration. One of my students, who was looking for a husband, wrote that she wanted a man who was worth at least ten million dollars, and had a house with a swimming pool. In New York City, the former is much easier to find that the latter. However, this girl was working as a clerk in a wholesale lumber brokerage, and the chance she would be able to meet such a man was very slight indeed.

When you are asking the universe for something, it is important that you consider your sphere of availability. This is what is actually available to come to you from the source of universal supply. Your sphere of availability is where those things you wish to obtain originate. This is what counts, those things the universe will grant you without difficulty. It is these things you may have from the source of universal supply, when you ask for them.

If you sincerely want something, you should only ask for what is within your sphere of availability. Should you ask for something that is outside your sphere of availability, you are very unlikely to receive it. This is a very important point, as while both men and women may have the occasional opportunity to enter briefly into areas where they might not always be welcome, they are unlikely to be able to remain there, and much less likely to move there permanently.

As an example, many very well off men, and a great many celebrities, will have an occasional fling or a 'one night stand,' with a woman they have met casually. In the process of seeing the woman, should the affair continue, the man may expose her to a lifestyle that she will be unable to attain over the course of her life. In some cases, the woman can read a great deal more into this kind of transient relationship than the man intends for her to see in it. He may believe that friendship and occasional sexual contact is a possibility, but she may believe that marriage is in the offering.

This fling with a wealthy man has not expanded the woman's sphere of availability, although it may well have expanded her greed to permanently live and attain the lifestyle she once so briefly enjoyed. Understanding this truth may be emotionally crushing to the woman.

You must study yourself and honestly attempt to determine just what your sphere of availability may contain. If in your list of requirements, you are asking for something that you become aware is beyond your reach, you should strike it off your list. Seeking something the universe will deny you will guarantee that you will not receive what you wish. In addition, you will possibly miss gaining those things you want in your list that are actually possible for you to have.

Improving Your Job Prospects

The idea that there is a non –physical component of every physical thing on this earth is certainly not a new concept. Primitive people all over the world supposedly knew it. However, it is something that few people living today seem to have ever heard of. I was not taught this idea in school, and I doubt you were either. Nonetheless, this concept is absolutely true.

If you were aware of this, has it ever occurred to you that you could use this information to your advantage? Until my teacher told me that I could, the idea of doing so had not occurred to me either. However, this information provides us a useful technique for integrating and advancing ourselves in any workplace, or any other kind of organization. It also allows us to become better adapted to any physical enviroment we may ever find ourselves in.

The knowledge there is a non-physical component of every organization or other physical and non-physical entity on this earth can be used for the benefit of anyone wishing to make use of it. The very fact that people do not know this is what gives the one who does have this information a tremendous advantage in their life. Over the last sixty years I have spoken with many spirits of companies, societies, courts, buildings and many other physical and non-physical entities. I have only very rarely come across the spirit of any one of these entities that has ever previously been talked to, shown interest or affection, or communicated with in any other way, by anyone at all.

Take a moment to think about the idea of communicating with the non-physical entity of the company you work for. Consider the idea that you might make friends with it, and hold regular conversations with it. As you become friendly with this entity, can you see that it might favor you as a part of the organization that it represents? This is exactly what I am proposing you do, to expand your relationship with the non-physical reflection of the worldly entity that employs you.

Of course, you may go much further and expand this idea to include making friends with the non-physical entity of the building you live in, as well as with the spirits of whatever social organizations, business organizations, or other entities, either physical or non-physical, you may contact in your daily life.

As you contact these non-physical entities, and as they gradually begin to recognize you as someone who is concerned about their welfare, they will reach out to you in the same friendly manner in which you approach them. In this way, the emotional and mental energy you expend communicating with them, or by paying attention to them, will soon be returned to you in a beneficial manner. The increasing rapport you have built between these non-physical entities and yourself can have only good effects for you over the course of time.

Greeting the Doorway

In some so-called primitive cultures, the recognition of the invisible forces that are reflections of the material world are taken for granted. Thus, I have heard of the practice of 'Saluting the doorway,' or 'Greeting the doorway,' which is to be done when entering a house. In this case, a set phrase is usually spoken when entering any house or building. For example, 'Peace and Blessings to this house and all within,' is one of several phrases that may be used. Another is, '(I give) Greetings to the door of this home.' There are several phrases used in different cultures, all with the same intent, to recognize the non-physical spirit of the doorway, and thus the non-physical spirit of the house.

While it is probably a good idea to recognize your own residence in this way, you can go far beyond this in recognizing the non-physical part of both your home and your employer. The method I am suggesting is useful for contacting the non-physical part of any organization or any physical structure you may have any connection with at all.

Speaking With The Spirits Of Organizations, Buildings, Or Physical Locations

Sit comfortably and relax yourself. Address the spirit you wish to communicate with by saying:

"I address my words to the spirit of the Millville Manufacturing Company." ...

Or for another example,

I address my words to the spirit of the building located at 12 Penfield Street in Paris, Illinois.

Or another

I address my words to the spirit of Palmer Lake.

Now pause briefly. Then continue speaking in a calm, slow, measured, and relaxed, tone, saying something like the script below. .

"I would like to build a friendly relationship with you. As _____ (The spirit of XXX)_____ you are important to me. (Give one or two reasons, 'Because _____') You are an important part of my life. I would like to become your friend."

Continue on in this vein, developing a friendly relationship with the spirit in the same manner you would use to develop a friendly relationship with a small child. Avoid being either intellectual or philosophical in your approach, and do not speak down to the spirit. Be quite plain spoken at all times. You can praise the spirit for some outstanding feature of the entity that it actually possesses, such as a leading position in business, or the outstanding architecture of a building but you cannot and must not lie to the spirit about anything. If you tell the spirit an untruth, it will know it, and your chances of ever developing a friendly relationship with it will be greatly reduced. Stick to the facts, and those things you know are true about the entity. Praise the facts, but do not flatter.

Once you have finished your first session speaking with spirit of the entity, you may end the session in the following way:

"I dismiss the spirit of ___(Entity)___ and ask the blessings of almighty God upon it, now and forever."

Those who may have read my book Mental Influence [3] will recognize that this is very similar to the procedure used in working with the sub-conscious minds of living people. The major difference is that using candles for protection is not necessary, as inanimate physical objects rarely strike out at people, and in the case of someone coming to them to develop a relationship, the likelihood of any natural entities striking out at the person addressing them is extremely small.

If you wish, you can think of things to talk to the spirit about. I will warn you that your conversation with the spirit will be very one sided until the spirit accepts that you are actually interested in developing a relationship with it. In most cases this will take some time. If you are talking to the spirit of your work place, you should mention interesting things that happened at work that day, and speak favorably about some of the people who work there. Until you have a good two-way conversation moving, and know how the spirit of your work place feels about the different people you work with, you should avoid criticizing anyone. The person you criticize might just be a favorite of the spirit of your work place for some odd reason of its own.

I assure you that this is an excellent method of situating yourself in your job and greatly improving your prospects for retention or even promotion. It has worked very well for a number of people.

---

[3] Published by Xlibris, Inc Philadelphia, PA in 2002   To purchase a copy call 1 - 888 - 795 – 4274 Or on the internet at Xlibris.com or Amazon .com

Improving Your Guidance In Life
By Praying To Your Guardian Angel

Just as you can profitably communicate with the non-physical entity of the organization that employs you, you will also find it personally profitable if you regularly communicate with your guardian angel, who is responsible for giving you the guidance you need in your daily life. Just as most people ignore the non–physical entities of the business around them, most people ignore the non-physical entity that is responsible for guiding them in life. This entity, or being, is often referred to in the Christian religion, as well as in several other religions, as the person's guardian angel.

A weekly prayer to your guardian angel will correct the deficiency of ignoring the important entity that gives you constant inspiration and guidance. The simplest way of showing your respect for, and interest in, this entity is through using the short prayer ritual given below.

Light a plain white candle, the kind known, as shabbats candles are ideal. They are often sold in grocery stores in the ethnic foods section. As the candle burns, pray the following prayer. When you have finished praying, allow the candle to burn out.

'You who are with me in this life as my guide and protector, I light this candle to thank you for your constant loving care and guidance. I ask Almighty God to bless my guardian angel.' Amen

Many people have reported receiving very positive results from reciting this prayer every Monday morning, as they begin their week. Usually they have recited this prayer for three or four months before they begin receiving more clear inspiration and guidance. Some people have used this prayer continually for several years, and believe they have profited greatly thereby. It is certainly worth your while to use this simple prayer regularly for at least six months, to see if you can receive the kind of benefit from it that most people using the prayer report they have received.

You may ask your guardian angel for assistance with specific problems, but until there is a two-way communication going on, you should not expect a verbal reply. Often the solution to the problem you mention will just appear, or it may possibly come to you in a dream. As with developing friendships with all non-physical entities, you must take time and be patient.

SPELLS FOR PROTECTING YOUR HOME

Many people use alarm systems, smoke detectors and a variety of other things to protect their home from physical problems. Few people ever think of spiritually protecting their home from the negative influences of others. However, the non-physical protection of your home is probably as important as its physical protection. Once your home is protected against non-physical assaults, your domestic life will be less influenced by the thoughts, jealousy, and envy of other people.

There are a number of simple ways to protect your home, most of which do not let others know you have done so. For example, in some Mediterranean countries, people paint their windowsills blue to discourage spirits from entering through the windows. People in these countries recognize this as a protection against evil, and assume the rest of the house is non-physically protected in the same way, although often it is only the windows that have been protected.

One of the more concealed methods of protecting a house is to ring the house with a small band or ocher, red iron oxide. This may either be done by painting a band of the red iron oxide paint around the foundation, or by sprinkling the ocher powder on the ground, as you walk around the house. Either way is equally effective. The red ocher powder or paint may be purchased at, or ordered from, an artist's supply or paint store.

A similar method of protecting a house involves sprinkling a band of salt around it. If you are sprinkling the salt on the bare ground you should be careful, as salt can do serious harm to any flower beds and plants you might have around your home. There are a number of other sprinkles you can place around your house, with the intent to protect it from harm.

There are also a number of plants which can be planted in any flower bed you may have around the foundation of your house, St. John's Wort being one of the most effective. Sunflowers, marigold, and several other plants are equally effective in protecting the home. You can check the influences you fear most and then see which plants best protect against them in a good herbal. I much prefer St John's Wort and Queen Elisabeth plant, although not all people find them pleasing plants to have in their garden.

The idea that you can simply pray for protection and have it instantly granted you is quite a charming belief. Unfortunately, it is also untrue. Although daily prayers for the non-physical protection of your house are worthwhile, it is also beneficial to take frequent actions to keep your house non-physically clean. Once again, this is a matter of trusting in God, but tethering your camel first.

The specific influences you may face will determine just what must be done, but mopping your floors with ammonia in the scrub water and adding a small amount of ammonia to the drains every night will be of great assistance. (A tablespoon of ammonia in each of the drains in your house is usually sufficient.)

Keeping your house calm, through the action of boiling a teaspoon of cinnamon every month, as mentioned in the first chapter of this book, will go a long way toward discouraging negative influences and malefic spirits from visiting your home.

If you have had a relative pass on recently, you should add their name to a glass of water and place it upside down at your door, using the spell mentioned previously, for the three months immediately following their death. This acts to keep their spirit out of your house, so they do not try to bring you to them.

Various powders may be added in small quantities to paints used to paint the walls of your home. Even Cinnamon and clove, if finely powdered, may be added to the house paint, used to paint either the inside or outside of your home. In addition to these powders, there are a number of magical powders that may be made and used up for specific things. For these you should consult a spiritual practitioner.

A Spell For Firmness In The Land Or
To Remain On The Homestead

The two following spells are taken from the book 'Magical Spells Of The Minor Prophets,' a book of bible spells that was published by Lulu in 2008. I am repeating them here word for word. I once used this first spell below to prevent a foreclosure sale Brooklyn.

Required: Dirt from the land the person casting the spell desires to remain on.

Spell: Pray the Spell over the earth three times, and then place the earth in the approximate center of the land.

Verse: Amos 9:15
15   And I will plant them upon their land, and they shall no more be pulled up out of their land which I have given them, saith the Lord God.

To Stabilize Someone In Their Home

Required: Four small pebbles, whitish colored pebbles are preferred. A saucer or dish, a shot of rum, whiskey, or vodka, a white candle.

Spell: Place the candle in the center of the dish. Place the four pebbles in front of the candle. Light the candle asking God's blessing on the home and those who live in it, naming each of them by name. Pour the liquor over the stones, and pray the verse on them. Again, ask God's blessing on the home, and those who live in it naming them by name. Allow the candle to burn out. Take the pebbles and place one in each corner of the house.

Verse: Obadiah 1:17

17   But upon Mount Zion shall be deliverance, and there shall be holiness, and the house of Jacob shall possess their possessions.

Spells For Vengeance And Revenge

Although the Bible clearly states, 'Vengeance is mine sayeth the Lord,' we oftentimes wish to take vengeance, or revenge on someone we feel has wronged us. Even though we may realize this might be a petty response to the problem, which in some cases may even be a problem of our own making.

One such desire for vengeance is stirred by being evicted from an apartment that we have occupied for some time. In New York City, evicting some one from their apartment, for either real or imagined reasons, is a common means of raising the rent on an otherwise low rental apartment that a person has occupied for some time. In such a case, I personally feel that taking revenge is perfectly justified.

Over the years I have heard of many ways of taking revenge on supposedly greedy landlords. These range from placing fish in the air ducts, allowing them to rot, to painting the walls of the apartment with black paint. Of course, if the landlord can prove you were the culprit, this often results in their suing you for the considerable damages that rectifying the situation your desire for revenge has resulted in. Only someone with nothing at all to lose can safely take such radical and destructive steps to gain revenge.

I understand there have been several books written that describe such physical means of disrupting the normal life of a home or apartment after an eviction or foreclosure. Aside from these efforts, which may cause the one who does them a great deal of trouble, there are a number of magical techniques that can be used to cause difficulty to the person who next occupies the home or apartment, and thus result in difficulty and inconvenience to either the landlord or the mortgage company.

Naturally I prefer these more subtle magical techniques to placing plaster of Paris the toilet, putting ready mix concrete in the sink and floor drains, or doing something else that might be physically destructive of the premises and result in a law suit.

Graveyard Dirt

Dirt from a graveyard, especially dirt taken from the grave of a friend or relative, is a very useful magical ingredient. Some years ago, one of the New York City supervisors of markets decided that graveyard dirt sold in occult stores in the city was a fraud, because it was 'just dirt.' Well, of course it is, but it's dirt from a graveyard, and often from a specific grave.

There are many ways of gathering or taking this graveyard dirt, and some of these procedures have elaborate rituals attached to them. However, all of these procedures have one thing in common, should you wish to have the spirit of the person in the grave actually do some work for you, it is necessary that you pay them when you take the dirt.

If you are sufficiently sensitive, you can go to a cemetery and ask the spirits there if there is anyone who can assist you in your difficulty. Then you should clearly explain your difficulty to the spirits, and ask again for their assistance. Should you find a helpful spirit ask the spirit to lead you to their grave. It is from that grave you should then ask the spirit for permission to take some of the dirt.

If you do not believe you are sufficiently sensitive, and have no friend or relative's grave from which to obtain the dirt you desire, you should walk among the graves until you find one of a soldier, and take some dirt from that grave. You should pay for the dirt by leaving a dime in the grave, pressing the dime a finger depth into the earth. You may also pour a shot of whiskey or rum on the grave, or even on the tombstone, doing whatever you may feel inclined to do.

I have found it useful to tell the spirit at the grave what I wish them to do, and then ask them if they are willing to do it. Once I have their agreement, I then take the dirt, pay them for it, and take the dirt home and prepare it for use.

Using Graveyard Dirt

A friend of mine explained the techniques he used to place what amounted to a curse on an apartment he had been forced to vacate. He obtained some graveyard dirt and made a hole in the wall, about a quarter inch in diameter. He put some graveyard dirt in the hole, and then patched the hole just as he had patched the other holes in his wall where he had hung things on the wall.

In the bathroom of the apartment, he found the medicine cabinet was held in place by two screws. He removed the medicine cabinet, and placed more graveyard dirt in the space in the wall behind the medicine cabinet. He told the spirit that it would be all right for it to spy on anyone using the bathroom, or anyone who might be sleeping in the adjoining bedroom.

My friend then took the remaining teaspoon or so of graveyard dirt and added an equal quantity of red pepper. He sprinkled this powder all over the floor of the apartment, as he was leaving it for the last time. As he did this, he prayed that the spirit would be energized and be active in the apartment, punishing anyone who tried to remove it from the apartment, which was now to be its playground.

Much later on he heard from another tenant that the apartment he had occupied was considered to be haunted now, as people living there heard strange noises and had other inexplicable events occurring to them. My friend commensurated with his former co tenant, and said nothing about the work he had done. However he felt that was a satisfactory answer to the landlord who had evicted him.

Some Further Uses Of Graveyard Dirt

Graveyard dirt can be mixed with red pepper, black pepper, and any other desired ingredients. This mixture may sprinkled on the floor of the entryway to an apartment building. As these entryways are usually open, it is difficult for the building management to keep you from sprinkling this powder there. People stepping in this mixture may have whatever difficulties you have asked the spirit to give them, but it is better if you pray over the dirt first, directing the spirit to inflame the particular person you wish to anger, or to afflict that particular person in some way.

In the event you are interested in a private home you can place the dirt on the steps, in the driveway, or on the porch. You may even wish to spread graveyard dirt along a walkway, sidewalk, or alleyway.

You can also add a little alcohol to the dirt to empower it further. If you are using a half-teaspoon of dirt for a particular thing, adding one or two drops of rum or whisky is usually sufficient to empower the dirt. This may be done whether or not you add any pepper or other ingredients, but you should do this before you pray over it. .

Goofer Dust

Made from graveyard dirt, sulfur, powdered rattlesnake skin, and several other interesting ingredients, goofer dust may be purchased from some occult supply stores. It is used to lay curses, and literally ruin the lives of those people it is directed against. Should you be able to purchase some, as many stores will not sell it to those they do not know, be careful with it, as it can mess up you or your family as easily as it could mess up the office of the mortgage broker who sold you that bad mortgage.

This material has many uses, and a number of people say that it does not have to be prayed over to work. I do tend to pray over things, although I have discovered that goofer dust ' does not respond as easily to directions given it as graveyard dirt does. This is one of the reasons I caution you in its use.

If you know where someone you truly dislike works or lives, you can sprinkle some of this powder where they are sure to walk over it. It may well have a devastating effect on them. It had a tendency to turn the life of the person who it is intended for to ashes, something that you should bear in mind before you use it.

Using Goofer Dust

Goofer dust may also be place on the seat of the person's chair at work, lightly sprinkled on their papers, or a tiny amount may be placed in an envelope and mailed to them. The goofer dust will act in the same way no matter how you apply it.

Nonetheless, the way you apply these magical powders is ultimately very much up to you. Use your inspiration and creativity to apply the power as you beleive it will have the best effect for you.

According to Ms. Catherine Yronwode of the Lucky Mojo Curio Company, some people sprinkle a bit of the powder on a letter they are sending someone, and then snake their fingernails in a zigzag lines down the paper while projecting their anger into the letter. They believe doing this places the vibration of the powder, and their anger, into the paper, without leaving enough trace of the powder to arouse their victim's suspicion.

Her book, 'Hoodoo Herb And Root Magic' is the authoritative text and reference book on afro-American Hoodoo magical practice. I believe anyone interested in natural magic should own a copy. Ms. Yronwode also has an excellent correspondence course dealing with hoodoo practice, as well as a web site on the Internet that has an abundance of information for anyone interested in natural magical practices.

The Theory And Practice
Of Working Magic With Symbols, As Well As With
Word And Number Squares

The concept of working magic with word and number squares is based on the animist idea that there is a non-physical spirit or 'intelligence,' of some kind connected to each of the particular symbols or squares being used. This spirit or intelligence is thought to be intrinsic to each of the many possible symbols or word or number squares. The squares and spirits are individualized in such a way that the symbol or square may be used to call or summon the specific spirit connected to that combination of signs, shapes, words, letters, or numbers used in forming the symbol or square. The spirit may then be asked to perform whatever work is in the nature or the domain of the spirit connected to that particular symbol or square.

Fortunately, most 'magic symbols or squares,' of whatever type, reveal their domain of influence in the written description that accompanies them, either in the accepted idea of the symbol, the text of the book in which they occur, or otherwise. Alternatively, you could call (summon) the spirit of the symbol or square and ask it what it might be interested in doing for you, although this is usually believed to be a less certain way of working, but it is presumed to be the way the descriptions of the squares found in books were originally obtained.

Probably the best-known repository of word and number squares used for magic is the book 'The Sacred Magic of Abramelin the Mage,' better known as 'The Book of Abramelin.' This book is available in two translations, an incomplete one made by S. L. MacGregor Mathers, in the nineteenth century, and a new, more complete and accurate rendition from George Dehn and Steve Guth, published in 2006 by Ibis Press in Florida. The whole book of Abramelin consists of four books, only three of which were translated by Mathers from the abbreviated French manuscript he found in the Library of the Arsenal. The explanation, the folk spells, and the initial theurgic work do not concern us here, as we are only concerned with the word and number squares, which are given in the fourth book. According to the author, these squares are useful in summoning the spirit to which the squares are connected.

The theurgic work, given in the third book which takes eighteen months to complete, is done to have another spirit, or even several spirits, become attached to the magician, both for his assistance and his guidance.

While many of these letter and number squares are balanced letter constructions, like the Sator Square, not all of the word squares of the Abramelin book are constructed in such a balanced manner. Some squares seem to be made of mixed or possibly random letters, having an unknown source. The meaning of the words used in these squares, if in fact they are words, is obscure at best. While the original language of the Abramelin book was German, it is quite possible that the letter squares were originally written in Hebrew, Arabic, or some other language. Some of these squares may be more ancient than even the fifteenth century origin claimed for the original Book of Abramelin.

There seems to be a generally understood belief that the letter and number squares in the book of Abramelin may not be used correctly by anyone who has not undergone the eighteen month theurgic preparation, and through that attained the Knowledge and Conversation of their Holy Guardian Angel, which is the object of this long theurgic operation.

Another, and possibly more rational way to put this is that people will not be able to gain from the use of these squares unless they have been able to demonstrate some competence and ability in the practice of magic in other forms. I would say that this latter is more probably correct. Using squares of letters and numbers is only another form of the art of magic. It is certainly not the only form.

A very small sample of the many squares found in the Abramelin book include:

```
M O R E H
O RI RE
R I N IR
E RI RO
H E R O M
```

Square One, Book One, Chapter One, 'To Know Past Things'

We shall balance this square with the succeeding square:

N A B H I
A D A I H
B A R A B
H I A D A
I H B A B

Square Two, Book One, Chapter One, 'To Know Future Things'

Using The Abramelin, And Other Number Or Letter Squares, In Magical Operations

The process of using number and letter squares for their specific purpose is simplicity itself. First, it is necessary to determine if the work may actually be accomplished. In other words, you have to know that it is physically possible to accomplish whatever it is that you wish to do. Building a bridge to Hawaii from San Francisco is impossible, so are a great many other far less complex tasks, some of which at first glance may look to be possible. Asking for the impossible is silly, as if you are asking for something that cannot be done, your reputation as a magician will suffer among the spirits, and the inhabitants of the non physical world will ignore you. In this case, your reputation and abilities may collapse even before you are well started on your magical career.

Make certain that what you ask is possible, and be sure you think about this seriously. You must think of how what you desire to happen might possibly occur. If you cannot think of several ways it might happen, it is most likely an impossibility, and you should not waste time asking for it to happen.

~-•-~

The magic squares of the seven major planets of antiquity are well known, and have been repeatedly published all over the world. As a result, there is a rather large thoughtform that may be used in dealing with each of them. This large and powerful thoughtform acts to encourage, and practically assure, the opportunity of success for the person who uses these planetary magic squares to assist them in casting spells relating to the rulership of the planetary spirits.

We have, for example, the magic square of Saturn, which is used for restriction, confinement, negation, coagulation, concretion, and all of the many other aspects of the affairs of Saturn.

```
816  618  492  276  294
357  753  357  951  753
492  294  816  438  618   etc.
```

These variations are all the same magic square, as can be seen by inspection. How many other varieties of this magic square can you make from these numbers? Are all of these variations connected to the same non-physical planetary influence? It would take some experimentation to learn the truth of this, would it not? However, it is certainly an idea for the experimentation of an interested magician.

-~-~-

One of the best-known letter squares used in Magic is the famous SATOR Square. It has been used for everything from a medical aid, to a domestic fire extinguisher. This square had been found everywhere, from inscriptions on walls and lead plates in ancient Rome, all through the Middle Ages, where it was used for a wide variety of purposes, to the present day.

In parts of medieval Germany, this square was once used as a fire extinguisher. Homeowners were required to have a prepared square on hand, usually painted on a wooden disk or platter. It was to be cast into a burning building to put the fire out. Naturally, there is some question as to whether these magic squares actually worked for that purpose.

However, the Sator square has not lost its charm; it is presently included in a variety of modern day magician's books. This square has certainly had a long and varied career. Even today it is said that the house that has this square placed in the center of the building, and at its highest point, need never fear damage from fire.

Used primarily against conflagration, The Sator Square has also been used in everything from love spells to sealing prayerful letters pleading for assistance from the creator. It is certainly one of the oldest and best known of all magic letter squares. This ancient magic square is still in everyday use today. Many people still believe that it is quite effective as a preventative against fire or other disaster.

```
S A T O R
A R E P O
T E N E T
O P E R A
R O T A S
```

Aside from squares, there are also a number of other letters and number arrangements used both in the practice of magic, and in 'traditional,' or folk healing arts. One example of these is the ABRACADABRA triangle used for some centuries to decrease fevers in both children and adults. The triangle is carefully and prayerfully written out on paper, with the intention that as the letters disappear, one at a time, so the fever will also disappear. The completed triangle is placed on the child or adult, often by using a string to tie it around the neck, the point of the square aimed down. When it is used in this way, the fever is supposed to be gone by morning. The fever is supposed to gradually fade away, just as the letters of the word disappear one at a time.

```
ABRACADABRA
ABRACADABR
ABRACADAB
ABRACADA
ABRACAD
ABRACA
ABRAC
ABRA
ABR
AB
A
```

A similar triangle used both as a medical preventative and for healing, is expansive rather than diminishing. This triangle is said to work effectively against blindness, so the triangle itself increases, allowing the sight of the person who uses it to increase over time.   As with the former triangle, the following one is to be prayerfully written out on paper and affixed to the clothing of the afflicted person. It may be written small and placed as a charm on the person who has poor eyesight or on someone who is developing cataracts. They are expected to wear it for some time, so the charm may have to be replaced should it wear out or become damaged in some way.

This charm is not as popular as the Abracadabra charm, possibly because it is not as well known.

```
S
SC
SCH
SCHI
SCHIA
SCHIAU
SCHIAUR
SCHIAURI
SCHIAURIR
SCHIAURIRI
```

~-§-~

Magic With Symbols

It may not be obvious, but symbols of organizations may also be used as aids in summoning the spirit of the organization in magical operations. The symbols of well known publicly funded organizations, such as the Red Cross, and Salvation Army may be used to guide relief workers to areas needing assistance, as one example. The symbol is used to summon the spirit of the organization, and the spirit is told of a particular need, as in the case of someone needing assistance due to flooding. The worker usually receives an inspiration to search out the recommended location, and the needed relief is soon provided.

Well known corporate symbols may also be used in this manner, but as the spirit of most organizations may be summoned without the use of symbols, the symbol is only used to give assistance in summoning, it is not a requirement.

~§~

Asking The Proper Question
The Hidden Key To Horary Art And Divination

When seeking information you also must know how to phrase the question you wish to have answered so that the answer will make sense to you. This is something that you also have to think about rationally. You should just jump to conclusions over the questions you wish to ask. The process of asking the proper question is always one of the more important points in any form of divination. For example, in dealing with the future, you are always better off to ask, "What will be the result of my doing X?" Experience may have taught you that it is quite possible for you to do many things you should not even have attempted to accomplish. I have found myself in that regretful situation more times than I wish to recall.

As an example of asking a confusing question, simply asking if Mike and Lucy will marry might well produce a Yes answer because Lucy will eventually marry Howard, and Mike will marry Patricia after a few years time. Asking, 'What would be the result of Lucy and I marrying,' might give you the rather discouraging answer, "Divorce, or misery" as easily as "Bliss and Joy." Thus armed with the knowledge of what the result will be, you can make your choice in the matter.

Do not expect long-winded answers from spirits. If you get a word or two you will have to interpret it as best you can. You should prepare for short succinct answers, and consider that when you are phrasing your question. Asking a question that requires a long-winded answer is usually a waste of time.

The answer to a question such as, "When will Lucy and I make love," is easily misinterpreted. The specific question, "When will I take Lucy's virginity," is also not sufficiently specific to gain the answer you seek, as the lovely maiden you adore may not, in fact, be a virgin. If you ask instead, "When will I have satisfactory vaginal sex with Lucy," you must bear in mind that the answer may be never, because the sex will possibly be unsatisfactory. Asking, "When will I have vaginal sexual intercourse with Lucy," is more likely to produce a useful answer.

It is vitally important that you phrase the question properly, as you will ultimately have only one chance to ask it. Repetitively asking the same question is the fastest way to discourage and chase away a spirit that is sincerely trying to fulfill its god given function by truthfully answering your honest questions.

The next consideration is whether the question you are asking is actually worth asking. It is far easier to research the date of Waterloo in a book than it is to ask a spirit. Idle or silly questions will soon bore any spirit to tears, and cause them to depart from your presence. Then you have lost the value of the square you have been using.

The final consideration is whether the spirit can actually accomplish the task you have set for it, in this case providing you a useful answer to your question. If you ask for the chemical composition of the atmosphere of Venus, you may well receive an answer, but it is quite likely you will not understand it. Your frames of reference, earthly symbols, and understanding of chemistry, and that of the spirit are certainly going to be very different. As a result, their answers to questions of this kind may be far different than what you desire to hear. This is one obstacle. Another obstacle is that the information you seek may actually be unavailable to the spirit, to you, or to anyone else. Some information is impossible to obtain, especially those things that are actually divine secrets.

You must always carefully think through any questions you may wish to ask, and you should take the time to gain some understanding of the possible answers you may receive. This must be done before you begin asking any questions of the spirit at all.

Phrasing questions is an art in itself, and it requires that you already know at least a little something of the answer, or possibly something of what the answer you will receive might be.

~-~

The Process Of Asking Questions

As far as the process of asking these questions using symbols and squares are concerned, first, the squares you desire to make use of are to be clearly written out. They should be carefully inscribed on white paper, although I see no difficulty at all in printing them on a computer printer.

The square to be used is placed on a flat surface, the writing up, and the spirit of the square is summoned and asked the specific question the magician wishes to have answered. I have always liked the phrase, "I summon, stir, and call thee up." It seems to me to represent the epitome of summonings, as it quite literally says it all. Naturally, you may use that or whatever other summoning phrases you desire.

In the case of the two squares given above, the answer to the question appears in the mind, as an appropriate offering is made to the spirit of the square.

During the initial summoning of the spirit of the square, it is possible to ask what offering is desired for answering the question. A candle or possible two or three candles are usually sufficient, although a glass of water, wine, or some other alcoholic beverage may also be requested by the spirit. The offering is best placed in the middle of the square being used, along with a statement that it is for the spirit attached to that square.

I will add here that the spirits of the letter and number squares of the book of Abramelin do not seem to have been used very often, despite the great reputation the book of Abramelin has for performing fearful and powerful fetes of magic. I wish you well in working with them.

Magic With Dominos

While on the subject of using symbols and squares for magic, we should not overlook the art of using dominoes in this way. They are an example of a commonly used symbol that have a body of thought attached to them. So they are also a well-known symbol, of the kind that may be used to perform magic.

Because there is a good sized body of belief that certain dominoes relate to certain things, reveal certain indications, or show certain results in a reading. This means that dominos have accumulated about the same astral force – or have developed a thought form - as many of the Goetic entities that are worked with in the Sixth and Seventh Books of Moses and similar works. In addition, it means that dominos may be asked to work for you, just as other non-physical entities, characterized by active thought forms, may be summoned and asked to perform some kind of work for you.

Should you have a set of dominos, you can easily perform this kind of magic for yourself. To work magic with your dominos, set out a domino whose spots reveal the influences you wish to call toward yourself, or to place on another person. You may identify the proper dominos you might for the influence you desire from the book 'Yoruba Domino Oracle,' the only book I know of that has a list of the meanings of single and double dominoes given in it.

Place a candle on either side of the domino, or dominoes, and light them, asking the spirit of the domino to attend you (And thus summoning them by any means you desire), so that you may make a request of it. You may place a small glass of water opposite you, on the other side of the domino. The presence of bubbles forming in the water will indicate to you the presence of the spirit of the domino who is attending you.

Once you believe the spirit is attending you, make your request of the spirit. Your request must be of the same nature as is shown by the nature of the domino, or dominoes, as they are used in divination. After making your request, wait patiently and see if you have an impression of what the domino spirit might wish to have in payment of the request. That having occurred, promise that you will provide such and such as the spirit wishes, once you know the task you have set the spirit has been completed.

Allow the candles to burn out. Leave the arrangement of domino, water, and candles sitting there until you learn the task you have set for the domino spirit has been completed to your satisfaction.

Once the task has been completed, you must pay the spirit what it has asked for. Usually this is only a glass of wine, or two or three additional candles. If you beleive the spirit is asking too much for the work, don't conclude the agreement. You are concluding a contract with the spirit. If the spirit does the work you requested, you must pay the requested price you have agreed to pay, no matter what it is.

For example: The five three domino augurs for a quiet and peaceful month, with some minor positive advancement, but nothing spectacular. It's a good first spell to use when beginning your work with dominos.

Should you desire such a calm month, set that domino between two candles and pray: "Spirit of the five three domino, I pray to you to assist me in gaining and maintaining calm and peace in my daily affairs for the coming month. If you succeed in this, I will offer you two more candles and a glass of wine in thirty days."

At the end of the month, if things have gone as you asked, you should offer the two candles and glass of wine in the same location you placed the candles you used to begin working this spell.

Astrology And Magic

If you are going to become a ceremonial magician, you will have to become an astrologer. There is no way around it. It is a perquisite to mastering ceremonial magic. If you are going to perfect yourself in any other form of magical practice, mastering astrology is not usually required, although it is often recommended. However, there are a few things you should know about the various sun signs, regardless of your desire to practice astrology.

Whether you are interested in becoming an astrologer or not, you should pay some attention to Astrology. All of the twelve Sun signs have both virtues and faults. It is worth looking into astrology to learn something about this.

~§~

Nonetheless, the most important part of applying astrology to magic is found in the Timing of Magical Operations. We shall only introduce the reader to this important subject. Additional study of Astrology is required to master the interesting and useful Astrological art of Calculating Elections.

Timing of Magical Operations

The timing of magical operations is often considered to be critical to the performance of the magical act, whether spell, ritual, or summoning. Thus it is to the advantage of those who wish to perfect themselves as magicians to perfect their knowledge of the means of properly timing magical acts and procedures. In fact, this perfection is most easily obtained by gaining some passing insight into the nature of astrology. No exceptional study is required, as the average ceremonial magician must familiarize himself with all of the fundamental astrological principals in any event. The most serious magical operations are most often based on the selection of the hour for their performance, a process known as forming an election, a branch of the astrological art devoted to choosing the best time for the work at hand through the use of astrological calculations.

Aside from the elections required for the most serious of the magical arrangements, there are also those minor arrangements, which come up from time to time, and do not require the services of a full search for an election. To suit ourselves for these magical acts, we need only to pay attention to the rules of the horrary art, another branch of astrology, and consider the aspects and application of the lunar orb. If this be done, with a clear view and no selfish mental distortion, we can see that we shall have increased accuracy in our minor efforts as well as in anything major that we may decide to undertake.

While the serious ceremonial magician will probably wish to have his elections perfected by one who specializes in that work, the rules of horrary art and common sense will make it possible for the ceremonialist as well as the beginner to undertake to time less extensive operations themselves. It is in the interest of this goal that the following material is presented to those who wish to become practicing magicians.

Firstly let us consider that the lunary sphere, that of the Moon, is that which is closest to the earth, and this is the depositor of the influence of all of the other planets on our terrestrial home. Now if the moon is void of course, there is unlikely to be an agreeable outcome to our magical efforts. This is also found in the horrary art, where the outcome of those things done under the void of course moon are said to be without a predictable ending. So let it become our first consideration that no magical act be attempted with the moon void of aspect in its course. This condition is so widely followed that most astrological calendars have the Lunar void of course times indicated on them.

We have further agreement with this should we wish to consider that the sublunary world is affected in its emotions and feelings by the course of the moon in the heavens. While we may wish to credit this to the female of the species more than the male, we find that it affects the male as well, especially as it acts on their desire to work or accomplish. For there are none of the children of Adam who are exempt from the influence of the emotions, no matter how staid they may seem to be. In fact, it is often found that those who seem to be the most unbendable in their straight path may collapse in time as something strikes them that shatters their façade, and renders them a tearful mess of the hysterical kind expected only of women.

So let us first consider the moon, and ascertain that it is in its courses, and then follow the advice of Pickatrix and judge its relationship by aspect to the Malefic, Mars and Saturn. If our proposed work is benefic, there must be no aspect to the Moon from Mars of Saturn. If our proposal is malefic, we shall seek out such aspects as a time to conduct our work. Those being ascertained, let us then seek out a time when we have either Mars or Saturn void in their courses, if we are proposing a benefic work, or making an evil aspect to the moon if the work we are involved in is malefic.

This simple guide will serve the beginner reasonably well, although it is not sufficient to guide the more complex operations of magic. For that a more detailed knowledge of Astrology is required.

Some Magical, And Other, Myths Explored

FOUR THIEVES VINEGAR
And Some Spells Using This Wonderful Magical Ingredient

Being The True Story Of Four Thieves Vinegar

During the black plague, which swept through Europe in the 1400's, some towns were overwhelmed with the number of dead. In many European towns, as many as 35% of the population died from the dread bubonic plague. Gravediggers died even as they buried the dead. In one town in southern France, there was soon no one left to bury the dead. The municipal authorities decided to release some of their prisoners to bury the dead, promising them freedom when the plague had passed, if they left town and did not return.

It came about that four thieves who had been arrested, tried, and sentenced together were released to become gravediggers. They cheerfully accepted the terms of release, in which they were to bury the dead until the plague had passed, and then they would have their freedom. In the fullness of time, the effects of the plague waned, and the four thieves were told that they could go free, so long as they left the town forever.

The magistrate, wondering how these four men had managed to avoid the effects of the plague, questioned them about it. They told him that they had obtained red wine vinegar, and added garlic to it, allowing it to rest for a week. They had each drank a wine glass of the garlic vinegar each day with their meal. Thus this mixture became known as four thieves vinegar.

A few spells using this useful ingredient have been mentioned previously. The procedure for making the four thieves vinegar is very simple. Take a bottle of red wine vinegar, and fill it with garlic cloves that have been peeled and split in half. Allow the bottle to stand for a week, and then drink a wineglass, two ounces, each day. It is possible to make up several bottles of this mixture, allowing one or more to rest while another is in use. The mixture is a natural antiseptic and possibly even an antibiotic. In addition, it also makes a tasty salad dressing. It is very protective and healing when used as a tonic. Naturally, this useful mixture also has a number of uses in magic. Some of the more popular magical uses are given below.

GO AWAY SPELL - Using Four Thieves Vinegar

Get a bottle, and place in it the name of the person you wish to rid yourself of written on a piece of paper. Add a tablespoon of four thieves vinegar (Or fill the bottle with it). Pray over it that the person be taken out of your life. Now go to a swiftly moving river or stream, and cast the bottle in it, praying again that the person be taken out of your life.

A CURSING SPELL - Using Four Thieves Vinegar

Get some chimney soot, some table salt, and some four thieves vinegar. Get a shallow dish or saucer, and put a tablespoon of salt in it. Add a teaspoon of the chimney soot, and mix it well into the salt, using a knife or a spoon, until the salt turns black. If the soot does not turn the salt black enough, add more soot until it does. Do not use more than a tablespoon of soot to a tablespoon of salt however. (Three teaspoons equal one tablespoon)

Once the salt has been turned thoroughly black, put the black salt into bottle, and add three tablespoons of Four Thieves Vinegar to it. Put the cap on the bottle and mix it well with a vigorous shaking. Mixing the material using the name of the person who is to be cursed, as indicated below.

"I mix this black salt and vinegar to curse the _____ of ___n._n.____ . Let it come together to make their life as barren as the salt, and as black as soot. May this mixture curse them. May they be cursed for _____ (days, months, years)."

Once the mixture is well mixed, take it to the victim's house. While praying your curse over it again, pour it on their front steps. Then throw the bottle in their yard and return home by a different way than you came to them.

Some Additional Spells
From the late Papa Jim Sickafuss

A Prayer To The Spirit Of Good Luck

This prayer is for all kinds of good luck, of whatever nature desired. It should always be prayed before gambling, especially by the woman of the house if she is going out to play bingo, or the lottery.

Mysterious spirit that directs all the courses of my life. Descend unto my humble home, illuminate me as my guide through the confused secrets of the lottery. Grant me the prize that is to give me fortune, and with it happiness, and the well being that my heart will receive. Observe that my intentions are pure and good-hearted, and are directed in a manner to do good, to help me, and to assist all human beings in general.

I am not ambitious for richness, so that I can be egotistical and a show off. I only want the money to buy my peace of heart, to help the ones I love, and to better myself.

I carry the symbol of a horseshoe, with the words good luck, and I call upon thee to do justice for me at all times.

Powerful spirit of luck and fortune, if you think that I should still pass many days on this earth, suffering the inconveniences that destiny sends forth to me, do what you will with me, as I resign myself to your wishes. If it is written in the book of my destiny that obstacles come into my life, may they be satisfactorily attended to and overcome. My voice implores thee with this prayer, expressed with all sincerity from my heart.

Amen, in Jesus Name
Now say your request and make the sign of the cross.

A Prayer To Win The Lottery

It is required before you go to bed, you are to pray devotedly the following prayer. After that, you should place a copy of the prayer under your pillow.

Mysterious Spirit, who directs all of the threads of my life, descend upon my humble residence. Guide me to find, by way of the secret chance of the lottery, the prize that will bring me fortune, goodwill, and rest. Penetrate my soul and examine it. See that my intentions are pure and noble. That they go forward for my good, and that of humanity in general. I do not want the riches only to be selfish. I desire the money for the peace of my soul, the virtue of my loved ones, and the prosperity of my enterprise. If I am one of those selected for the lottery prize, indicate to me the number, which my ticket should have. Amen.

This prayer should be said at the same time every day
It is a seven-day prayer, even if you should win the prize before it is finished!

Before you pray. Take a bath with one blue ball, after you take the bath, light one jumbo green candle that has been rubbed with Saint Jacob oil. As you rub the candle, think of your winning. Then light the candle, and burn some Abtina Incense. While the candle and the incense is burning, say the above prayer and then the Lord's prayer three times.

When you go to the gambling make three crosses on your chest with Indian Good Luck perfume, and make one cross on your forehead, and a cross on the palms of your hands.

ITEMS NEEDED:
    4 jumbo green candles   Prayer   7 blue balls (chalk)   Saint Jacob Oil   Abtina
incense   Indian luck perfume

Some Myths And Misunderstandings About The Occult

Charging For Occult Work

The well-known Christian occultist Dion Fortune, stated that it was adamant that "it is an axiom of occult science that no price may be charged for any form of occult work." Her words, and her views, were thought to be correct in her mind, but they are certainly not universally applicable. Nevertheless, she charged a decent fee for admission to her Society Of The Inner Light, the occult organization she founded. I believe there was also a monthly fee for her continuing lessons.

She also believed that the Cabbalah that system of the much-modified Magical Octagon, altered in Moorish Spain for use in Jewish meditative worship, and known as the Cabbalah, was the fountainhead of Western occultism. Naturally, this completely ignored both Celtic wood magic and the use of Norse runes, which were far more widely used in Fair Albion at the time the Cabbalah was first introduced to the educated of Europe by the writings of the Jesuit Kirchner, Europe's first scientific superstar. It seems Miss Fortune believed these were both negative practices.

I don't know if she believed in the so called law of the three fold return of spell work, but in her memory, and following her lead of plunging in when historical blindness reigned, we can probably assign that to her as well. Doing so would give her the requite three errors proving 'the sophomore syndrome has fully grasped a hold of her mind.'

~-~

Belief and faith enter into the practice of both religion and magic to a remarkable degree. Like the queen in 'Alice in Wonderland,' most people find it quite easy to accept the idea of agreeing with, if not firmly believing in, 'ten impossible things before breakfast each morning.' Thus, learning something that is supposedly secret, these self-proclaimed students of the mysteries pass it around in whispers until it breaks out into the light of the sun as if it were a fully verifiable fact, when in fact it still remains only nonsense.

Of course, none of the three beliefs given above are even remotely true.

First off, considering the true nature of these so called occult sciences, in which the blind lead the blind, while the wise look on with either amusement or despair, there are certainly neither rules nor axioms in the real fabric of the occult that can be applied to those who are fundamentally playing with scraps of rumor and belief, while entertaining themselves with the idea of gaining great power. Let us look at these ideas singly, just to see if any of them can really hold any of the rare drops of the water of truth.

FIRST – The idea that no price may be charged for any form of occult work negates any number of beliefs, beginning with the idea that a 'workman is worthy of his hire,' the fundamental postulate of all economic systems. We may ask how it is expected that the person doing the work may eat and pay his daily living expenses. Is he supposed to have coin magically come to him? Is the occultist expected to work hard at some mundane task so that he may pour out his non-physical abilities upon the heads of the demanding, critical, and unappreciative 'great unwashed?'

There is never any lack of people seeking miracle workers, and a lifetime of observation has shown me that these wonder seekers immediately become quite uncaring and indifferent toward the one who has helped them, once their time of crisis is past.

Naturally this does not prevent these people seeking out the wonder worker, should something else trouble their self-indulgent hearts. There is no lack of those seeking free work of any kind, not just those seeking magical remedies to their current problems.

One of my students set out to become a Tarot card reader, having mastered the ability to read the cards to a degree that satisfied me. She was quite successful reading the cards for donations in Washington Square Park. Having proven her competence to herself and the universe, she began seeing clients, and charging a reasonable fee for her readings. After a few months, she came to me in disgust, saying that many of her clients thought she should be willing to correct those spots in their life where the course of their existence did not run smoothly enough for them. She added that none of them had offered to pay her any additional fee for performing these additional services for them, even assuming it were even possible for her to accomplish such often miraculous changes.

This is but one of the reasons I discourage those who wish to do so from becoming spiritual practitioners. It is not a profession providing either wealth or the promise of an easy life. Additionally, one meets a number of poorly developed people, many of whom are only looking for someone else to blame for their lack of success in life. Additionally, if you rely on so called contributions, as many workers in the occult field seem to do, you will be amazed at how little people believe valuable information, often life saving to them, is worth. When my student was reading cards in the park, the average contribution she received was only a quarter.

SECOND – The idea that the Cabbalah is the foundation of Western occultism is a poor joke. The history of the introduction of the Cabbalah to Europe is proof enough of that. Once it was 'Jewished,' the cabala developed rapidly, as Mark Twain once said of the freemasons, 'growing rapidly at both ends,' until it was said that God had personally taught it to Adam. In fact, the date of the introduction of the Cabbalah to the Jewish community of Seville in 849 AD is known. The fact of the modification of the original system of the octagon to the ten sphere cabalistic system, accomplished to suit Jewish ritual practice and give God a minion, is also known.

The Roman Catholic Church destroyed with vigor any competing ideology, especially including all those of a spiritual or mystical bent, that it found anywhere in Europe. The Cabbalah, as expounded by Isaac Luria, found favor with the church. Under the guidance of the Jesuit Kirchner, it was able to fill this gap in the spiritual with some of his assistance. The idea that the Cabbalah has any long history, or that it is the foundation of any form of the hidden mysteries, is laughable, except to those who are historically illiterate.

The Jesuits themselves were founded based on a mystical meditative practice of Arab Sufi's, taught to Ignatius Loyola while he was being held a prisoner of war in Moorish Spain. The present day spiritual exercises of St Ignatius Loyola are a modern simplification and weakening of the exercises that Loyola was originally taught by his jailers. Even so, they are worth going through for any Christian who wishes to develop himself spiritually.

THIRD – The idea that should you do an evil spell, the universe will return it to you with three-fold force is curious, but it happens to be absolutely untrue. The practice of thousands of primitive magicians, and other professional magic workers for hundreds of years easily proves this. I beleive this belief originates in one of those fearsome oaths taken as part of the initiation into some originally mystically oriented lodges and fraternities.

'May I be publically disemboweled, my intestines placed on a fire before my eyes, and my body cut in twain before my life shall perish.' This sort of thing as a threat is interesting, but I have never heard of any such thing ever being carried out by any of these lodges, which today are primarily men's social clubs.

Aside from the fierce oaths of these mystical and fraternal lodges, I have no idea where any of these foolish ideas of the automatic return of evil spells might originate. On the other hand, I know that for thousands of years generations of primitive people have cursed their enemies, often quite effectively harming or even killing them without any negative repercussions at all, save the usually return of the curse by being infrequently cursed by their enemy in return.

As to the idea that people believe these falsities, well, I can only say that in my experience, I have found that people will believe anything, if it pleases them to do so.

Melchizedek

Another interesting error that has carried on over time is the misinterpretation of some words in the holy scriptures of popular religions. One of the most misunderstood, or misused of these words is Melchizedek, the King of Salem. In fact, the correct translation of this phrase, which appears four times in the Holy Bible, is

'The Priest of Jupiter,' who is also known as the ruler of peace. (King Of Salem mans King of Peace)

Naturally, accepting this phrase for what it appears to be would indicate that a pagan priest was serving Abraham, who tithed to him. This introduces a potential religious conflict. That was not the intent of the original words at all. If we recall the context of the phrase, Abraham was returning from a battle, and this offering of bread and wine was to officially announce to all concerned that first, he had been the victor, and secondly, that he was now satisfied with his winnings and was once again at peace with the world.

Such after battle declarations of peace were not unusual in ancient times, and were still occasionally found among remote tribes as late as the nineteenth century. It is not at all unusual that it would be mentioned in the bible (Genesis 14:18) as a fitting finish to the battle against the kings, Abraham had just completed.

As being a 'Priest of Jupiter,' and by connotation, a 'Ruler of Peace,' was considered to be an honored title, it was also granted by the psalmist to his master, as in Psalms 110:4, where the master is praised with that title. We should expect that the giver of peace would be a priest, and that a priest would serve the most high, something stressed in Hebrews 7:1, at a time when the true meaning of the 'The Ruler of Peace,' had probably been lost. Thus the author of Hebrews gives this title to Christ, (Hebrews 7:15) considering it to be one of the higher appellations that could be given to a man.

The fact that later generations have adopted it as a title in their religion, or that some authors have adopted this name as their own is immaterial. Again this just shows a lack of education, as the Hebrew words making up Melchizedek are Melki meaning Priest, and Dizak, meaning Jupiter. This is something any Hebrew student can easily recognize.

Unicorns

The unicorn is known as a single horned white beast with a red head that is calmed and rested only by laying his head in the lap of a virgin.

Modem motion pictures and representations believe this was a horse like animal with a narwhale's horn protruding from his forehead. There is an even more interesting explanation of this ancient joke. Yes, for joke it is. Think about this white animal that has a single horn with a red head that is satisfied only by placing his red head in the lap of a virgin.

Is this not an accurate description of sexual intercourse?

When Alexander's armies conquered Egypt in the third century BC, he left a small garrison there as he continued his conquest of the world, as he knew it. The garrison was primarily concerned with the administration of the nation; along side the

Egyptian priests, who were the traditional administrators of Egypt. These Macedonian administrators were white skinned, and in many cases, blue eyed blonds. They were as strange to the Suntanned and black Egyptian fellahin as if they had come from the other side of the moon. Naturally, they went on inspection trips around the country. And naturally, they copulated with the many available Egyptian women who they stayed with in the various places they visited.

One of their compatriots among the party of Egyptians accompanying them probably first made up the joke about the white beast with one horn that was calm only when he could put his red head in the lap of a virgin maiden.

And thus the story of the unicorn (means one horn) spread and was accepted. It actually has nothing at all to do with horse like animals.

Gypsy Card Reading

This is why I don't believe in consulting Readers and Advisors. The following is taken from an instructional talk one of these readers gave me when she consulted me about a personal problem.

This is the 'Gypsy Street Method' of reading ordinary playing cards. It is done with a standard poker deck of playing cards, without any jokers. It assumes that you have memorized several lines of 'patter,' of the kind used in 'Black Gypsy Cold Readings.' The patter is used to fill in the spaces in your reading. When you give a reading you should always speak confidently, as if you were certain of what you said, and defiantly read it as a past, present or future event in the life of the person. The delivery of your reading, and the way you read for your client, is at least as important as what you tell the client.

(1)   Have the client separate the cards into three approximately equal piles. There
            should be approximately seventeen cards in each pile.
(2)   Have the client select one of these three piles. Pick up and quickly put away the
            other two piles. Get them out of sight immediately.
(3)   Have the client take four (or five – your choice) cards from the remaining pile.
            Turn them face up in front of the client, in the space between you
       and her.
(4)   Begin with the reading, based on the following guidelines:

Card Meanings

King of Hearts – The Male client or the primary male figure, or the lover when reading
for a female client.

Queen of Hearts – The female client or the primary female figure, or the lover when
reading for a male client.

Ace of Spades – Death or serious injury, depending on the supporting cards. When you
are reading this as death, you must note which cards are next to the ace of
spades to determine who this death pertains to. If it is the King of
Hearts when reading for a male client, or the Queen of Hearts
when reading for a female client, it is the client's death. If the
death of a client is clearly shown, it is best to want the client only
of 'the strong potential for an accident,' and urge the to take
great caution in their affairs.

Seven of any Suite - Relates to the client's home.
Eight of any Suite - Relates to correspondence of some kind, (including Emails.)
Nine of any Suite - Relates to thought, ideas, verbal communication, or education.
Ten of any Suite - Relates to Travel, a change of scene, and possibly a change of work.

The Suites Of The Cards Determine Their Value Or Impact

The red suites are favorable Diamonds relate to money - Hearts relate to Love

The black suites are unfavorable Clubs relate to trouble – Spades relate to serious injury,
illness or, as with the ace of spades, death. Spades always require that a warning
of some kind be given to the client.

Face cards deal with relationships to others. The suite of the face card
and the numeric value of the surrounding cards determine the relationship and
it's impact on the client.

Odd numbered cards deal with men, while Even numbered cards deal
with women.

As an example, in this reading: A three of clubs next to a ten of
diamonds indicates that, 'the reader sees there will be a trip involving money,
but there will be some trouble involved in either the trip or gaining the money.'

With a two of clubs, a little trouble, with the ace of clubs a great deal of trouble, etc. You must read the cards as they are surrounding each other.

Learn to read the cards as if you were reading a book, following the above guidelines. If you are not sure what you see, go with your first instinct. The cards are only a channel for your reading anyway. Learn to master listening, as the client will tell you everything you need to know. Watch the client's responses to what you tell them. Their body language will tell you as much as their words.

Most people do not want to hear about their future unless it is good. Most people do not have a good future ahead of them.

31,291

Made in the USA
San Bernardino, CA
29 November 2012